EP Sport Series

Tennis up to Tournament
Standard

Modern Riding

Sailing

Table Tennis

ep EP PUBLISHING LIMITED
1974

squash
rackets

This edition is
published in association with
SUCCESS SPORTSBOOKS
Published by
John Murray (Publishers) Ltd.

Tony Swift
National Coach of the
Squash Rackets Association

◄ the author

Acknowledgements

The author would like to acknowledge with thanks the assistance of the following in the preparation of this book:

Philip Ayton—featured on the cover photograph

Peter Verow for taking part in the action photographs

Ian Cook of the *Squash Player* for the photographs

Lambton S.R.C. for providing facilities for the photographs

Pictures by courtesy of the *Squash Player* International magazine

Dunlop for providing the equipment for some of the photographs

ISBN 0 7158 0584 3

Published by EP Publishing Ltd, East Ardsley, Wakefield, Yorkshire 1974

Printed in Great Britain by John Blackburn Ltd, Old Run Road, Leeds

CONTENTS

Preface by E P Woods

The Squash Rackets Association set up its coaching service some ten years ago and many have benefited from the work of those amateurs who have given up their time and effort for coaching. September 1st, 1972 was a notable date in the development of this service as it heralded the appointment of the Senior National Coach, Tony Swift. The responsibilities of the Senior National Coach are manifold; one of his earlier tasks was to ensure the production of coaching materials written and visual, which included such items as film, film strips, slides and coaching notes.

EP Publishing Limited, whose book "Know the Game—Squash Rackets" is a leader in the low price range of elementary coaching books, approached the SRA with the idea of producing a more comprehensive, better illustrated book on the game. The approach was timely and welcome because it fitted in with the Association's policy for developing material.

This book is the result of hard work and the co-operation of many people, clubs and organisations in producing something which was needed at all levels of the game; it is specifically directed at the beginner and the intermediate club player. It will be as beneficial to the coach as to the player—but as the demand for coaches is, and will for some time to come, be greater than the supply, the book will stand on its own as an instructor. The book will become your coach and provide an excellent means for any individual of any age to advance from a novice to a competent player.

The SRA is grateful to and loud with praise for all those who have made this book possible and so vital a part in the development of the game.

Foreword by J H Horry

Squash is basically a simple game and as such it could be argued that one can learn to play squash just as well from a book written 50 years ago as from a new book. But the game is changing with the new Australian dot ball demanding new techniques, and success at squash today is a challenge which every player consciously or unconsciously must accept. The vast majority of players have no ambitions to become a champion but they would like to improve their game sufficiently to ensure victory over the chap they normally play with. And this is precisely what this book will help every player to do.

Most books on squash are written by champions or ex-champions. Here is a book written by a player who is still improving his game by putting into practice what he preaches in his book. Tony Swift's advance from a hack county player to one who was knocking on the door of the England team was

achieved in the space of 3 years; unlike most ascending players he also found time to devote to coaching others. Now, as the National Coach, he writes with unquestionable authority. Moreover there are many players in Zambia, Kenya and in many other parts of the world who can testify to their improved play following attendance at his clinics and coaching sessions.

I don't think I have ever come across anyone (with the possible exception of Jonah Barrington) more dedicated to squash. Both Jonah and Tony have been my assistants so that I have had ample opportunity to observe them. Both had the enormous advantage of being coached by Nasrullah Khan, the greatest coach the game possesses, and in this admirable book Tony passes on many helpful hints which he learned from "Naz". It is impossible to teach the game successfully by word alone and the success or failure of a squash book

may well depend on its illustrations. This book is unusually well illustrated by action photos and will appeal to modern players.

In short, here is a book written by one who has won acclaim both as a player and as a coach, and with this book I feel certain that he will win acclaim as a writer as well. I commend it, not only to the beginner but to players right through the many grades of squash. In it there is something to help every squash player.

Introduction to The Game

The game of squash was first thought to have been played at Harrow School over 100 years ago. Schoolboys waiting their turn on the racket court used to knock up outside, but too many windows were broken by the hard ball. A soft "squashy" ball was then introduced and this transpired to be the start of the game as we know it today. Squash spread through the public schools and the Forces, and many courts overseas were built for Army officers serving abroad. However, the first real boom occurred in Australia in the early 60s. In a short time 4000 courts were in use. The Australian organisation is different from that in Britain; centres concentrate on the public court rather than the club and this means that players from all walks of life adopt the game.

The boom which Australia experienced has now reached Britain and there are well over 1,000,000 players playing on over 3000 courts.

The popularity of the game is rapidly spreading and in the next decade the boom will probably extend to Europe. The signs are already there. Sweden, for example, which had less than 10 courts 3 years ago now plans to build 80 courts in the next 5 years; already 50 have been constructed. In Finland there are growing numbers of keen squash players and the game has also started in Germany. There are now courts in Holland, Denmark, Belgium, Monaco, Greece, Italy, Spain, Switzerland and Portugal. The fact that the game is world wide and is played in over 45 countries, is reflected in the inauguration of the International Squash Rackets Federation in 1967 and the founder members were Britain, Australia, New Zealand, South Africa, Egypt, India and Pakistan. Previously, the game had been administered throughout the world by the British Squash Rackets Association. Since the foundation of the ISRF, individual and team championships have been played every 2 years and which are regarded as the official Amateur Championships of the world. It is interesting to note that Australia has dominated both the team and individual events since their inception.

But perhaps the most impressive explosion in the game will be seen in Japan in the next 5 years. It has been decided that squash will become Japan's national game and there are plans to build 7000 courts in the country during the next 5 years.

"Squash" has certainly become the game of the 70s. There are many good reasons for this, especially these days when people are so aware of the need to keep fit. Squash is an energetic game, and in a short time, a tremendous amount of exercise can be achieved. It is an enjoyable way of taking exercise, and "running off" the extra pounds as one chases the little black ball round the court. In half an hour one can have had more exercise than in a three hour game of golf or two hours of tennis. The time factor is a great point in the game's favour; business men find that they can have a game of squash, a shower and a quick drink in their lunch break—far better than spending 2 hours over a huge meal and too many drinks. Proof of this can be seen in the City of London where more and more brief cases have squash racket handles protruding from them. Squash is also rewarding to the beginner; novices can fully enjoy even their first time on court. Unlike lawn tennis, badminton, or table tennis, one does not need a good player on the other side of the net (or tin as it is called in squash) as the ball comes back from the front wall. For this reason, beginners find that they can play rallies and their improvement can be quite rapid. Once they realise how enjoyable this can be, and can see their improvement, they go back for more and their enthusiasm soars. It is an easy game for the beginner to play. Compared with other sports, squash is a cheap game to play, but in Britain, the biggest advantage is that it can be played at any time of the night or day and is never dependent on the weather.

Squash is a game of many standards, but provided one plays an opponent who is of a similar standard, whether it be a novice, an International or even a veteran (classed as over 45 in squash circles), a vigorous game with all the exercise expected, will be guaranteed.

To some people squash may seem only like chasing a little black ball around an enclosed space as long as one's legs last—usually long enough to induce a terrific thirst. But the serious player knows it is more like a game of physical chess.

The skill and strategy needed to place the ball as far from the opponent as possible in order to create a winning position, is something that only the experienced squash player can fully appreciate. This book is based on the recent series of Squash Coaching Films produced by Gerrard Holdsworth Productions Ltd and will serve as useful back-up reading material for anyone who has viewed the film. However the book is written as a coaching manual in its own right and is for all players who want to improve their game whether they are complete beginners who are taking to the court for their first few games, or club and county players who, despite what they think, often need to be reminded of a few squash "basics". The book not only looks at the shots used in the game, how and when to play them, it discusses practices, basic tactics, fitness training and a few rules of the game.

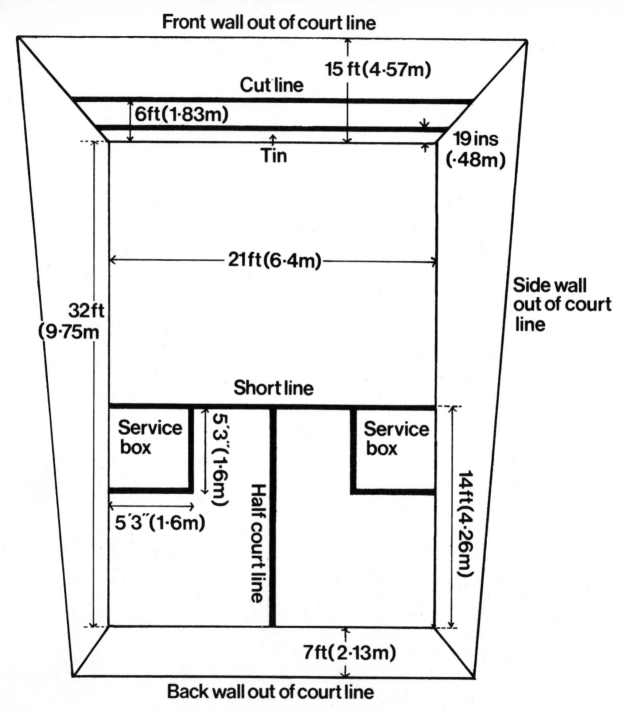

Front wall out of court line

Cut line

15 ft (4·57m)

6ft (1·83m)

Tin

19 ins (·48m)

21ft (6·4m)

Side wall out of court line

32ft (9·75m

Short line

Service box

Service box

5'3" (1·6m)

5'3" (1·6m)

Half court line

14ft (4·26m)

7ft (2·13m)

Back wall out of court line

It is the first squash book of its kind, in that there are over 130 photographs designed to supplement the text.

The Court

Squash is played in an enclosed rectangular room bounded by high white walls. Apart from the dimensions of every court which are standard, two courts are rarely the same. The roof height, which is not specified, can vary, as can its colour and the fittings which hang from it. The old courts often had a glass roof which would be a glaring mass when the sun shone in the day and a black holed cavity at night. The lights used to be tungsten filament lamps although these are now being entirely replaced by fluorescent tubes. Just as the height and colour of the roof determine whether or not a lob could be used to good effect, so does the position of the girders or beams supporting the roof, for if a ball passes over a

permanent structure or hits it, then the ball is out of court.

The walls are usually plastered and white, although precast wall units are now being used more often. Glass back walls, which have been successfully used on the Championship Court at Abbeydale Park SRC, Sheffield, are a recent

development, and they have made good viewing possible for much larger audiences. Who knows? Glass side walls suitably treated may be used in the not too distant future.

The pace of the court, in other words the speed that the ball travels round the court is deter-

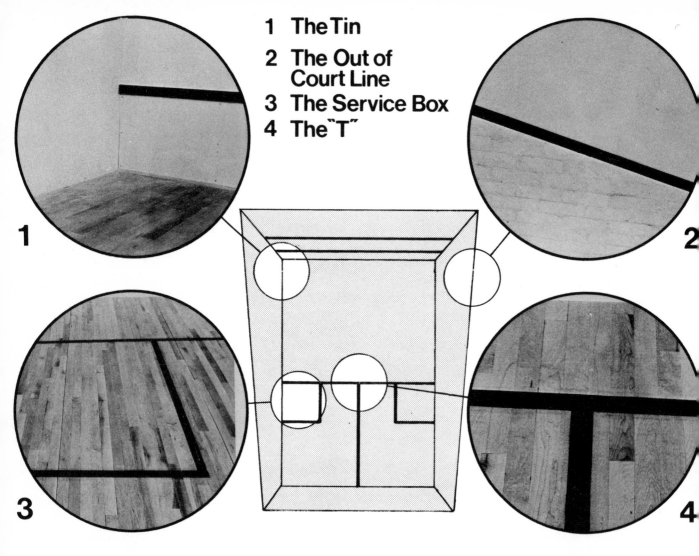

1 **The Tin**

2 **The Out of Court Line**

3 **The Service Box**

4 **The "T"**

1

2

3

4

mined by the wall structure, the temperature of the court, the surface of the strip wooden floor and the type of ball used. Canadian maple or beech is recommended for its light colour and hardness, and to protect the floor, sealer is sometimes used (although this can cause more trouble than it is worth if not applied properly). There are many variations which contribute to the individuality of one court, whatever the conditions, make use of them and adapt your tactics accordingly. The lines on the court need to be clearly understood. On the front wall the lower red line marks the height of the tin (similar to a net in tennis) above which the ball must be hit, while the top line running around the walls—the out of court line—is the boundary line and the ball must not hit it, or anything above it. The other lines all relate to service; the cut line in the middle of the front wall and the lines on the floor, the short and half court line (forming the "T" in the middle of the floor) and the service boxes.

In the UK there are over 700 clubs with more than 3000 courts. They are spread throughout the country though not surprisingly, most of them are in the densely populated areas of Surrey and Middlesex. If you have no clubs within easy reach it might be that your local sports centre—and there are more local authority centres being built than ever before—contains public squash courts which can be hired. A list of all affiliated clubs is published each year in the SRA handbook, available from the Secretary, Squash Rackets Association, 70 Brompton Road, London SW3, price £1 inc postage. Also in the handbook you will find a list of professionals and approved amateur coaches to whom you may wish to turn once you decide to have expert tuition.

How Points are Scored

The game can be likened to tennis except that both players are on the same side of the net or tin, as it is called in squash, which is a strip of metal at the bottom of the front wall. The players have a racket each and take it in turns to hit the black soft rubber ball onto the front wall above the tin and below the top line. The side wall and even the back wall can be used to achieve this, provided the ball does not hit the floor first. A player loses a rally if he fails to make a good return. A return is good if the ball is returned onto the front wall above the tin without touching the floor or any part of the players' body or clothing, before it has bounced twice upon the floor, provided the ball is not hit twice, or out of court.

A point is scored only when the server (known as hand in) wins a rally ; when the server loses a rally he loses the right to serve and the opponent (known as the receiver or hand out) becomes the server. This system means that one point can go on for a long time if the players alternately lose a rally, which will give two players of similar standard the exercise they are seeking. It also allows the server greater freedom in his choice of shots because a mistake will not cost him a point.

The first player to score nine points wins the game, and a match usually consists of the best of five games. If however the score reaches 8-all, then the receiver can decide whether the game is to be played to nine or ten points. The longest game would therefore be 10-9.

Equipment

Those who play tennis or badminton can use the same clothes and shoes for squash, although obviously the racket and ball are different. However for those who have not played other games there are essential items which you should have in your squash bag which can itself take various forms from a brief case to a special bag designed to hold squash kit and rackets.

The Shoes

The shoes are probably the most important part of your equipment. All squash players run on their feet and as there is much twisting and turning in squash it is essential to have comfortable shoes. If you have ever tried playing with corns or blisters you will know what I mean. The requirements of a good shoe are a balance of good grip (by the sole), support and flexibility, and it is a help if they are light. Shoes must have a white sole otherwise court-

owners will not allow their use on the light coloured maple squash floors, as the soles mark the wood.

Socks

White socks should be the thick cushion foot type, since they are comfortable and will absorb sweat, but do wash them regularly, not only for hygiene but unwashed socks are guaranteed to cause blisters. As to the size, make sure they fit, allow room for your toes to move, do not have them too small or too large.

Clothing

Freedom of movement is essential in the clothes you buy, which according to Rule 25 should be white. Ladies allow themselves coloured trims and motifs on their dresses, but too much colour is unfair as it can be distracting and if it is a dark colour the black ball can be "lost" occasionally. Your clothes should be absorbent as you will sweat on court, profusely at times. A sweater is useful, not only for the cold courts which you will play on, but to keep you warm after a game on the way to that well-earned shower. The surest way to catch a

"severe" cold is to cool off and
stand around in the cold before
going to the shower.
Keep your clothes clean and
ironed; the better you look, the
better you feel and the better you
play!
Hairstyles have changed, and it is
the men who are wearing headbands
nowadays—these help to keep the
sweat and hair out of your eyes, and
additionally you may like to use
wrist sweatlets to prevent the sweat
dripping into your hand.

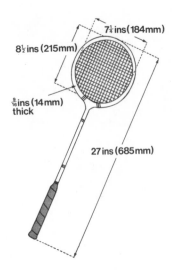

7¼ ins (184mm)

8½ ins (215mm)

9/16 ins (14mm) thick

27 ins (685mm)

The Racket

A racket is probably the most expensive item in your bag, but like your shoes, it is equally important. Having decided on the price you wish to pay, it is then a matter of personal choice but in deciding there are several points you should consider. The handle can have a towel or leather grip (a short or the more conventional long handle) the shaft of the racket can be wood, fibre or metal, although the head must be wood. The stringing varies from nylon, superlastic or gut, the latter is used in all top grade rackets and it can be strung loosely or tightly. The balance and weight of a racket varies, it can be light or heavy in the head and as with the other variables it is a matter of personal preference, but try each type, have a few "swings" in the shop and see which you prefer. A head cover is not a bad idea if your bag is not large enough to carry the racket.

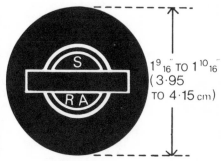

1^9_{16} TO 1^{10}_{16}
(3.95 TO 4.15 cm)

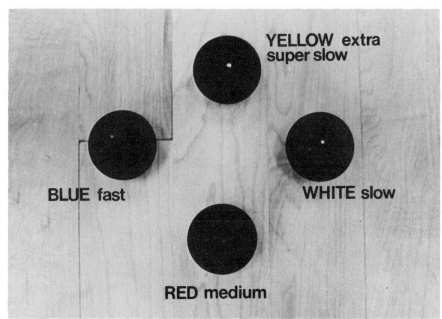

YELLOW extra
super slow

BLUE fast

WHITE slow

RED medium

The Ball

There are 4 balls available, each of rubber. They differ only because the temperature in courts varies enormously round the country. In London the courts are often situated next to kitchens or heated swimming pools, consequently they are very hot and a slow ball is preferred by the players. However there are courts in the provinces which have outside walls and in mid-winter it is like playing in a fridge—a faster ball is needed. The 4 speeds are indicated by a coloured dot on the ball. The yellow dot is the slowest; then white, red and blue dot the fastest. Whichever you choose make sure it suits the courts and if in doubt ask someone who knows the court better than you. It is also important to choose the ball to suit your standard of play, a faster ball should be used by beginners. The more experienced player should know that most championships in the UK are currently using the yellow dot ball. However much research is being carried out to find a universally acceptable ball, one which plays well and does not mark the walls. This is necessary when one realises that the

Australian and British balls differ in composition and bounce. A ball which does not mark the wall is now also available and has been accepted by the court owners but not so readily by some of the players. In general then use the ball which gives the best game on your particular court.

Lastly there are a couple of items which you might like to include in your bag—ladies will find it useful to have a couple of safety pins for the inevitable strap breaking, while the real enthusiast will have a skipping rope for the 500 skips after every game ! The hypochondriac, of course, will be able to produce a chemist's shop from his bag but all that is really necessary is a plaster to protect the odd blister.

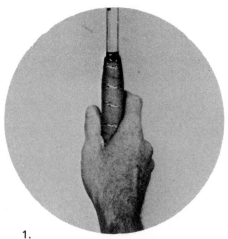

1.

The Grip
The grip for squash is known as the "shake hands" grip. In other words shake hands with the handle as though you were shaking someone's hand.

The thumb and forefinger form a "V" which points up the shaft of the handle, and the fingers which are spread very slightly grip the racket lightly but firmly.

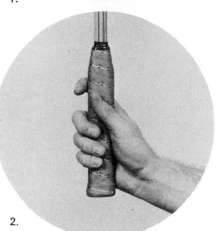

2.

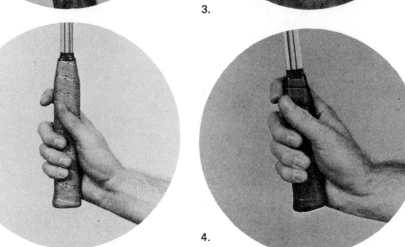

3.

4.

5.

1. Correct grip
2. with a long handled racket

3.⎫
4.⎬ Correct grip with
5.⎭ a short handled racket

Racket face slightly open

The racket should not be held so tightly that the grip becomes painful, as would happen if the fingers were clenched or clamped round the handle. The forefinger should grip the racket outside, *not* inside the thumb. The last 3 fingers and the inside of the thumb form the pressure against the handle, while the forefinger is used more for control than grip. The thumb lies across the shaft at about 45°, with the end of the shaft just protruding beyond the base of the hand. If the racket is being held correctly, with the shake hand grip, then if one imagines the edge of the racket head to be a hammer, it should be an easy and comfortable task to knock a line of imaginary nails into the floor in front of you. The same grip is used for all shots. The reason is that the ball travels round the court quickly and a player does not have the time to change the grip, nor is it necessary to change grip. But it is necessary to keep the racket face "open" to the ball and in order that this may be achieved the wrist in relation to the forearm is turned anticlockwise from a 2 o'clock position on the forehand to a 10 o'clock position on the backhand. The grip however remains the same as does the firmness of the wrist. The photographs show the grip of a right-handed player, and all references throughout the book refer to this player, as can be seen in the photographs.

The Swing

It is most important to have a good swing—not only will it allow you to hit the ball correctly but also, with two players in close proximity to each other, an excessive swing on any shot is dangerous. A correct, grooved swing is vitally important too for accuracy.

The swing is usually broken down into 3 parts.

The Backswing must be prepared early, to give you choice of shot, and to hamper your opponent's anticipation of the shot you are going to play. Arriving to play the ball with the back swing up also enables you to delay the shot so that he is often left flat footed. Failure to prepare your stroke in this way makes it likely that you will snatch the ball and hit a hurried and uncontrolled shot. To ensure the swing is not excessive, bend the elbow; the racket shaft must be held vertically with the wrist cocked, forming a right angle with the forearm. This angle is maintained as the racket is pulled down to strike the ball, only with this angle is it possible to get any real racket speed on striking the ball.

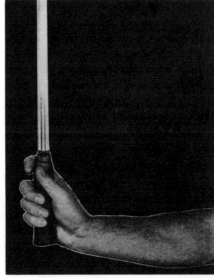

The cocked wrist

The extent of the backswing varies but top players on the forehand could bring the backswing so far back, to gain maximum racket head speed, that the head of the racket can be seen out of the corner of the left eye, with racket shaft horizontal. However it would be sufficient for beginners to start with the racket shaft vertical, bending the hand back to ensure a cocked wrist, keeping the elbow bent.

After the initiation of the downswing, the racket face must remain slightly open before, during and after impact.

At impact the ball should be struck level with the leading foot, with the weight of the player having been transferred onto the leading foot. At this point the racket head passes through the flat path at maximum speed along the line of the intended flight of the ball. The flight path of the ball at the top of its bounce is also flat; make it easier for yourself by hitting the ball at the top of the bounce, keeping the racket shaft horizontal and the racket head level with the wrist.

If the ball does not bounce very high, then bend the knees so that the ball can still be hit with the racket head level with the wrist, don't drop the racket head to meet the ball. A dropped racket head causes the wrist to become loose

23

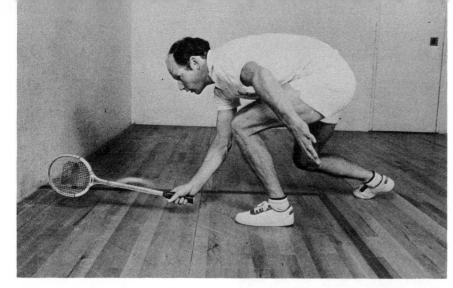

Hitting a low ball

(a) A correct follow through
(b) Incorrect follow through which is an excessive swing

and there is a tendency for the swing and the shot to be played from the wrist, and not from the arm as it should be. The point of impact for normal purposes is at a distance from the body by the length of the almost extended arm and the racket.

The swing on the forehand is completed with the **follow through,** the racket head ending past the players left ear. The elbow is bent with the racket shaft finishing almost vertically upwards, elbow bent again. A straight arm is one of the commonest causes of the excessive swing, which is dangerous to the opponent. When moving round the court remember it's the racket head that does the work and hits the ball. Watch any top player and you will see that the first thing that moves when he makes a movement to the ball is the racket head. So help yourself by keeping your **Racket**

a

b

Head Up during a rally. Remember there are several advantages in holding the racket head up:

1. Because the time required to play the backswing has been reduced it allows the player more time to play the shot.
2. It allows a shot to be delayed, thereby fooling your opponent.
3. It gives you time to choose which shot you are going to play.
4. It enables you to go further into the back corner of the court to play a shot without fear of hitting the wall.

Geoff Hunt (Australia) uses the racket head as deception in his match with Hiddy Jehan (Pakistan)

Basic Shots

correct:
racket face
slightly open

wrong:
racket
face closed

The Forehand and Backhand Drives

These shots are used more than any other and the forehand and backhand drives provide the basic length game. In each case the shot should be played with a firm wrist with the racket head level with the wrist when the ball is struck. The face of the racket should be slightly "open" so that the ball travels up onto the front wall. If the racket face was closed the ball would travel downwards, with the likelihood of hitting the tin.

◀ Backswing of the Forehand Drive

The Forehand Drive

This is the first basic shot in squash.

1. The backswing starts with the racket head near the right ear, with the forearm parallel to the floor, the elbow tucked into the body so that the racket shaft is vertical. In this position the wrist is "cocked" ready to play the shot. Experienced players would extend their backswing backwards from this position to gain maximum momentum of the racket head on the downward swing (as discussed in the swing).

2. The left foot is moved forward in the direction of the right hand side wall so that the body faces the side wall.

3. As the racket head is drawn down the body weight is transferred from the right (back) foot onto the left (front) foot.

Ken Hiscoe (Australia) with a typical
approach to a Forehand Drive. Racket
head being drawn down from the
Backswing

(a) Impact
(b) Follow through

a

b

4. The ball is struck at the top of
its bounce level with the left hip
and at a comfortable distance
from the player, with an open
face and having the racket head
level with the wrist; so that the
racket shaft is virtually parallel
with the floor. The racket head is
swung through the ball. If the
ball is struck either too close or
too far from the body then there
is a tendency for the wrist to be
used, and power and control are
lost.

5. To help keep the weight into the
shot, both knees and back
should be slightly bent. If the
player is too upright there is a
tendency to pull away before the
shot is completed.

6. The follow through is completed
with the racket head finishing
near the left ear, the racket shaft
returning to a vertical position
with the racket head up and the
elbow bent.

The follow through should not be
made across the body having the
shaft parallel to the floor with a
straight arm—this is known as
excessive swing and is dangerous
on a squash court where there are
always two players in close
proximity to each other.
The left arm is used for balance and
should be stretched outwards to
give freedom to the striking arm.

Correct: Bending to meet the low ball

On a low ball, the knees and back should be bent so that the ball can still be hit at the top of the bounce with the racket head level with the wrist. Don't drop the racket head to meet the ball.

The forehand is usually played in the right half of the court.

Dropping racket head to meet ball

Jonah Barrington, the winner of the 1973 British Open Championship, demonstrates good footwork, balance and follow through on the Forehand for a left handed player. It seems that all great players have a grip of their own. Hashim Khan, who won the British Open for seven years, held the racket half way up the shaft. Here Jonah holds the racket with a slightly unorthodox grip—note how his forefinger is inside the thumb

Backhand Drive
(a) Backswing
(b) Impact
(c) Follow through

The Backhand Drive

The backhand drive is similar to the forehand in many respects, the main differences being:

1. The backswing starts with the racket head above the left ear, except for experienced players who exaggerate the backswing and start with the racket head visible out of the corner of their right eye, with the racket shaft parallel with the floor. The right angle between the forearm and the racket shaft is maintained as the racket head is drawn down to meet the ball. Do not start the swing with a straight arm—the cause of an excessive swing.

2. The right foot is moved forwards in the direction of the left hand side wall so that the body is facing the side wall.

3. The body weight is transferred from the left (back) foot onto the right (front) foot, as the downswing starts.

Incorrect backswing—excessive

a

b

c

▲
Backhand drive

Incorrect: excessive follow through

4. The ball is struck at the top of its bounce but slightly in front of the leading right foot. In this way all the power can be transferred into the shot, as the racket face is swung through the ball, along a flat path.

5. The follow through concludes the stroke with the shaft nearing the vertical on completion of the swing with the racket head up. Failure to keep the racket head up can cause an excessive and dangerous swing.

Alauddin in play against Geoff Hunt during
the Semi-Final of the 1973 Open
Championship. The shot demonstrates the
good footwork, balance and follow through
after a low Backhand Drive
▼

▲ Hiscoe in the other Semi-Final against
Barrington in an almost identical
position to Alauddin

Above right: Hiscoe getting down to a ▶
low ball on the Backhand. Knees and
back are bent thereby ensuring all the
weight is in the shot

In both forehand and backhand shots the left arm is used for balance, while the grip is the same for both shots.

Footwork is the key to a good shot so be on your toes during the game, be nimble, so that you can move to your shots easily—don't be stiff legged.

The forehand and backhand drives should always be played to a good length, that is after hitting the front wall, the ball should bounce on the floor towards the back of the service box. On its second bounce the ball should die in the back of the court. In order to bring the drive to a length the ball should hit the front wall on or near the cutline—if it is hit too low, ie. just above the tin,

the ball will hit the floor in front of the short line allowing the opponent to move forward to play his shot, thereby putting him in a dominating position at the front of the court. The length shot will force the opponent to the back of the court, and the nearer the drive is played to the side wall the more difficult is the opponent's shot (any ball which clings to the side wall is difficult to play)—it also prevents the opponent from volleying the ball which he could do if the ball was played well away from the wall. The cross court drive can also be played as an alternative to the straight length drive. The forehand cross court drive would be played in the right hand court with the ball

being hit to the left hand court, ie. across the court. Similarly, the cross court drive on the backhand would be played in the left hand court, the ball being hit to the right hand court.

The forehand and backhand cross court drives are played in the same way as the straight drive, the only difference being that the ball is taken slightly earlier so that the ball is struck further in front of the leading foot than for a straight drive.

The follow through, of the racket head which takes the line of the ball after it has been hit, will be towards the middle of the court instead of parallel with the side wall. The completion of the follow through

Heather McKay (Australia) probably the
world's greatest woman player shows
perfect balance in her approach to this
Backhand Drive ▶

will be the same as the straight
drive, but make sure it is not
excessive by bending the elbow.
A common mistake made by
beginners when learning a cross
court shot is that they try to pull
the ball across the court by
pivoting their body with the
shoulders rotating as the ball is hit.
This is one cause of bad cross
court shots. Play the shot with the
body and shoulders stationary until
the shot has been completed.
The line that the ball takes after
hitting the front wall is important. It
can be appreciated that if the shot
is played from one back corner to
the opposite back corner the ball

The Forehand Drive played : (A) Straight
                            (B) Across Court

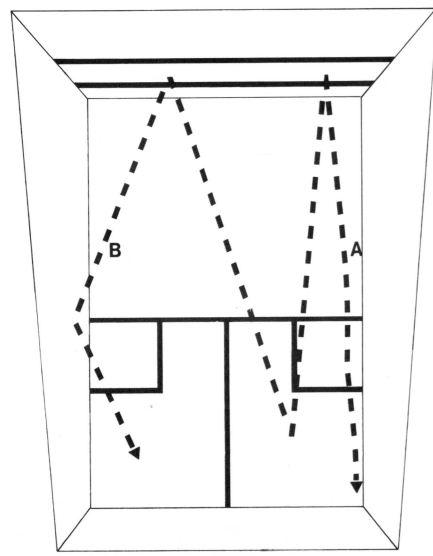

B   A

would make a "V" with the front
wall. This would allow an opponent,
positioned on the "T" to cut the ball
off as it returned from the front wall.
It is important therefore to make
sure that any drive played across the
court, **must be played wide** away
from the opponent. As a general
rule if a drive is played across the
court always play the ball so that
after returning from the front wall it
hits the side wall opposite where
the opponent is standing.
By playing the drive wide in this
way, you can achieve the following:
1. The opponent is unable to cut
    the ball off: it is too wide.
2. Instead he is forced to move
    back from the "T" towards the
    corner to play the ball as it
    rebounds from the side wall.
    Any ball which comes in
    towards the player off a side wall
    is a difficult shot to play—so
    his next shot has been made
    awkward.
3. He has been moved off the "T",

(On all line diagrams the dotted line indicates the path of the ball)

38

Correct position for practising the forehand drive

you can get on it.

It is important to practise all shots. When practising the forehand drive on your own stand behind the service box. Learn how hard to hit the ball and where the ball should hit the front wall to bounce in the back of the service box, dying on the second bounce at the back of the court.

Use the service box as your target area and count the number of times in succession you can make the ball bounce in the box. With continued practice this number will improve. One word of advice,

when practising don't try to hit the ball too hard too soon. As your ball control improves try to keep the ball down the side wall as close to it as possible, varying your pace depending on whether you hit the ball high and slow or hard and low, but always aiming for a length.

A similar practice can be used for two players; this time the players would practise their movement to and from the "T" after each shot, simulating in practice a game situation.

Of course the same practices could then be tried on the backhand.

The Service

The service is one of the most important shots in the game; it is not, as so many players think, just a means of putting the ball into play. It is important for three main reasons:

1. The service is the only shot in the game in which a player has complete control of the ball; every other shot is governed to some extent by his opponent's return. It is therefore possible to perfect a good service, and to take your time.

2. If the server wins a rally a point is scored by the server.

3. A good service can put the server into an attacking position at the start of the rally, by forcing the opponent to boast the return of service. Once the server has forced the opponent to boast the return of service, he can move to the front of the court in anticipation of the boasted return, to which the server replies with a straight drop shot as quickly as possible. The drop shot forces the opponent to move the full length of the court—one of the most tiring movements in squash.

The rules state that the ball before being struck shall be thrown in the air and shall not touch the walls or floor. The ball shall be served onto the front wall so that on its return, unless volleyed, it would fall onto the floor in the quarter court nearest the backwall and opposite to the server's box from which the service has been delivered.

At the beginning of each game and of each hand, or rally, the server may serve from either box, but after scoring a point (ie. by winning the rally for which he served) he shall then serve from the other and so on alternately as long as he remains in hand or until the end of the game. One realises immediately that there is a choice open to the server, he can serve from either the right hand or left hand box, he can serve on the forehand or backhand, hit the ball hard or softly and as the service boxes are 5' 3" (1·60 m) square there is some choice as to where he can stand when serving. I shall discuss the choices.

The Forehand Lob
(or floating service)

The most difficult service for your opponent to receive is one in which the ball is hit softly onto the front wall, hitting the front wall almost halfway between the side walls and not much below the top line, so that the ball rebounds from the front wall and floats down hitting the side wall just below the out of court line towards the back of the court. This is called the forehand lob service and is probably the most effective. First learn this service from the righthand service box, which is only an extension of the forehand cross court shot.

1

2

4

5

3

1. Preparing to serve
2. A good throw-up
3. Impact
4. Follow through—eyes
5. still on the ball

The rules state that one foot must remain in the service box until the ball is hit. In order to make the movement to the centre of the court easier after the service has been delivered, place the right foot in the box. The left foot is just outside the box, the line formed between the toes being the line which the ball will follow in flight to the front wall. Throw the ball from the left hand straight up into the air, about two feet, and as it drops swing the racket head up and through in the intended direction of the ball, with an open racket face. Hit the ball slightly in front of the body, at about waist height, keeping your body still until the shot has been completed.

Don't rotate your shoulders. The position of your feet means that you will be facing the front wall when serving from the R.H. box but face the right hand side wall in the L.H. box.

Footwork for the service and after the service is important. Ideally the best position to hit a lob is to stand against the front wall, hit the ball up the front wall so that on rebounding it drops almost vertically into the back of the court. But one foot must remain in the service box until the ball has been struck, so stand as near to the front wall as possible, that is at the front of the box. One can stand near the wall to make a wider angle for the cross court shot

Movement to the "T" — eye on the ball

but this necessitates an extra two steps when moving to the "T". Most players stand nearer the middle of the court so that in two steps the server can move to the "T". Do not move backwards after service, a player who moves backwards is likely to be on his heels and therefore off balance, but move straight to the "T", and keep your eye on the ball.

When serving a forehand service from the right hand box you will have your back to your opponent. Always look at your opponent before serving to make sure he has not moved his position at the last moment, as this could affect where you would try to hit the side wall. A lob service may be played from the left service box, but the angles are narrower as the ball is struck in the middle of the court. Care must be taken not to push the ball out of court above the side wall line.

The Forehand Lob Service from the
left hand box

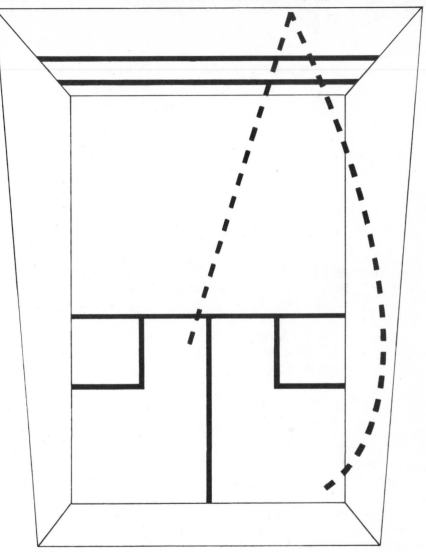

a quick look at the opponent before
serving

The higher and slower the ball returns from the front wall the more difficult the return, particularly when the ball is near the side wall.

1. If the opponent chooses to volley the return, he may hit the wall and miss the ball.
2. If the opponent prefers to let the ball bounce and the ball has been hit softly, it will not bounce very far out from the back wall, and the opponent will be forced to boast the return.

I prefer the floating service for three reasons:

1. It is easier to control.
2. It is difficult for my opponent to return.

3. It takes no energy to hit the ball—this is an important factor in a long hard game when conservation of energy is very important.

It is important to practise the lob service however, for a poor service enables the receiver to dominate the start of the rally.

The Forehand Hard Hit Service

An alternative service from the left box is the defensive serve. The ball is hit lower and normally harder on to the front wall, returning as nearly as possible parallel to the opposite side wall.

A third alternative is the surprise service, a hard hit ball aimed at the front wall just above the cut line, so that on rebounding it travels straight at the opponent. Such a service will take the opponent by complete surprise, having become accustomed to the floating ball, and there is every chance that he will miss it, but if he is lucky enough to connect there will be a fair chance it will fly straight into the ceiling. An easy point for the server.

Never be afraid to vary the pace and direction of your service, either for surprise, or if your opponent is coping well with one particular type of service.

One word of warning about serving when tired. Do take care. After a long, exhausting rally it is so easy to serve your hand out by hitting the ball out of court and so infuriating ! Take your time and serve more carefully.

The Backhand Service

The backhand floating or hard hit service may be used, and from the R.H. box it has the advantage over the forehand service, that the server can always see his opponent.

The footwork is different in that the left foot is the one which remains in the service box until the ball has been hit. The ball is thrown into the air and as it drops the racket head is swung up through the ball, hitting the ball with an open faced racket between waist and shoulder height. Having struck the ball, the server should then move onto the central "T" position as quickly as possible, **always** keeping his eye on the ball.

The Rules on Service

For the benefit of those players who do not know the rules on service it would be a good idea at this stage to discuss them.

In terms of the rules, a service is good which is not a single fault or which does not result in the server serving his hand out—a double fault.

There are various ways in which a service becomes a single fault:

1. When the ball hits the front wall above the tin but on or below the cut line.
2. When one foot at least is not grounded within the service box on striking the ball. The other foot can be anywhere provided one foot, or the part of that foot which is touching the floor, is within the box.
3. When the ball, on returning from the front wall, does not land within the opposite back quarter of the court.

A combination of any of these three faults on one service only constitutes a single fault.

If the server serves one fault, he will serve again unless the receiver elects to take the fault which makes the service good and allows the rally to continue.

Having served a single fault which the receiver decides not to take, the server has a second service which must be good. If however there is a let played in a rally started on a second service, then the rally is replayed with one fault still standing. The server serves his hand out, that is a double fault, and loses the stroke if he serves two consecutive single faults or:

1. When he serves the ball out of court, ie. when the ball hits the top line or anything above it.
2. When he hits any surface other than the front wall first, ie. the side wall, the tin, or the floor. Therefore if a server throws up the ball, strikes at it and misses it, and the ball hits the floor first it is a double fault! The other foot can be anywhere provided one foot, or the part of that foot which is touching the floor is within the box.
3. When the ball hits the server on returning from the front wall.

Return of Service

Just as the service is important, so too is the return of service. The player who plays the return of service is known as the "receiver", or "hand out". The receiver waits to receive service in a position of readiness, with the racket head well up, for an early preparation to any shot, and eye on the ball (not the front wall). His position in the back quarter of the court should allow for movement forward or backwards depending on the type of service. Most players normally stand in the middle of this quarter of the court, halfway between the back wall and the back of the service box. By standing too deep in the court near the back wall, the receiver will be forced to take the ball late in its flight giving the receiver ample time to dominate the "T", and the start of the rally.

Position of readiness

Positioning for service and return of service

On receiving service in the L.H. court, the return will be a backhand drive, volley or lob whereas in the R.H. court the return will be a forehand.

The return of serve should be designed to move your opponent from the "T" and this is best achieved in two ways.

1. A straight return down the wall to the back of the court (known as the length drive).
2. A high cross court return to where the server has served from, but wide enough so that the server is unable to cut the ball off from his position on the "T".

The importance of length on the return of service cannot be stressed enough. If the receiver plays the return short, not only is there a great risk that the ball will hit the tin giving an easy point to the server (one he hasn't had to work for at all) but even if the ball goes up, you have placed your opponent in an attacking position at the front of the court.

The return doesn't have to be hit as hard and low as possible to bring it to the back of the court. Far better to stroke the ball softly and high onto the front wall so it floats into the back corner of the court. Should the server manage to hit the side wall, the receiver's shot is made more difficult. The answer is to learn by experience to judge when the ball is best taken after it has hit the side wall. Then move backwards initially allowing yourself room to play the ball which will be coming in at you off the side wall, but moving forward finally to hit the ball. You should not be moving backwards when you hit the ball. The more experienced a player becomes the further forward he will stand, somewhere near the backline of the service box. The receiver is still free to move forwards or backwards depending on the type of serve received, but is better placed to attack a poor service. The more advanced players with good volleys move even further forward and often hit the ball from a position as near to the short line as possible. Their experience allows them to judge the flight of the ball quickly so that they can move back if necessary to play the ball, but the point of standing so far forward is that it puts the server under pressure before he has even hit the ball. He realises that if he serves a bad service the receiver can step in and volley the return so quickly that the receiver can move to the "T" and dominate the rally. The receiver may even hit an outright winner if it is a very poor service.

Therefore always try and volley the return of serve, this prevents your opponent from taking up his dominating position on the "T". The top Australian players, who are currently the best squash playing country in the world, are masters at volleying the return of serve and often gain this early domination of a rally.

In summing up therefore, a good service puts the receiver in a defensive position, allowing the server to dominate the "T" and possibly to move into a winning position at the front of the court. A perfect service may even win the rally outright. However a poor service allows the receiver to move forward and take the ball early, returning it to a length, allowing the receiver to dominate the "T", and forcing the server into a defensive position at the back of the court. The tactical battle starts from the very first shot in a rally. Each player tries to dominate the central "T" position. The service and the return of service, whether good or bad, determine who will dominate at the start of every rally.

Having learnt the forehand and backhand drives and discussed the service and return of service a beginner is ready to try a game.

However to make the game more interesting and to add variety to your play we shall discuss some further shots, how and when to play them before discussing tactics used in a game.

Attacking and Defensive Shots

We have discussed how a poor service gives the receiver an opportunity to attack the return. Often this will be by volleying the ball.

The Volley

The volley is a shot played so that the ball as it returns from the front wall is hit before it bounces on the floor. The ball must therefore be hit earlier than the drive so the racket head must be well up, not only for an early preparation to the shot, but to ensure a firm shot. If the racket head is not held up but dangles by the floor then by the time the backswing is prepared the ball has passed the player and the volley is missed. The value of the volley is that in taking the ball early its return from the front wall is quicker giving the opponent less time to prepare for his next shot. The opponent consequently is put under pressure, it follows therefore that the volley should be played as often as possible. Unfortunately to volley the ball often one has to be extremely fit to reach the ball early enough to play the volley, hence its lack of use.

Gogi Alauddin demonstrates an early racket head up

The volley then is used as an attacking shot and is usually played in the vicinity of the short line. It can also help you to maintain a fast pace against a player who prefers a slower game. The safest volley is one which is played to a length, with the ball going to the back of the court. It is also the easiest type of volley to hit, as the racket head is meeting the ball with maximum surface area, returning the ball back to the front wall along a similar flight path from whence it came, to ensure its return to a length.
If the ball is volleyed down towards the tin it is a riskier shot. Not only is the ball being hit down near the tin (it might even be hit into the tin) but the racket head will be coming down across the flight of the ball. Furthermore a volley which is played down onto the front wall will bounce short into the front of the court. Thus if it is not an outright winner, the volley played short has brought the opponent into the front

of the court and into an attacking position. To ensure it is a winner try and angle the volley so that after hitting the front wall the ball falls into the side wall near the front wall, and play the shot from the short line with your opponent behind you.

When hitting a volley try to keep the racket head well up for a firm shot. Ideally the player should face the side wall by moving the feet, as for the drives, but as the volley is played earlier it is often sufficient to turn the hips so that the upper body is facing the side wall as the ball is

The Forehand Volley
Impact

Follow through

struck. However beginners should concentrate on moving the feet to ensure that the body faces the side wall, only in this position can the ball be hit straight down the near wall to a length. The ball should be hit slightly in front of the leading foot at about shoulder height so that the player's weight can be transferred forward into the shot, which is a punch usually with a shorter backswing and follow through than for the drives.

The racket is held firmly with the same "shake hands" grip. On the forehand the weight is transferred from right to left foot into the shot while on the backhand the weight is transferred on to the right foot. A high backhand volley is a difficult shot to play; make it easier by using the left arm in a scissors action for balance and to help the explosion of energy and punch into the shot. Just as with the drives, it is important to practise your volleys. Initially try some volley practice with your coach then when you can hit the ball well, practise straight volleys on your own. Stand on the short line and hitting the ball above the cut line see how many consecutive shots you can hit on the forehand before trying the backhand.

One point to remember when practising any particular shot. If it goes wrong—stop, pick the ball up and start again; a small discipline which if applied in practice will

The Backhand Volley
(a) Backswing
(b) Impact
(c) Follow through

later be reflected in your game. In other words don't fall into lazy, sloppy habits when practising. Is one side better than the other? If so concentrate on the weaker side until both are as good as each other. Finally there are several practices in pairs for the volley—here are two. Firstly try a cross court volley practice, which combines a backhand and forehand volley practice. It is also a good practice to teach you to hit the ball wide when playing across the court. Learn to

Practising for the volley in pairs

move to the ball, with the racket head well up, so that the ball is hit at a comfortable distance and slightly in front of the body. The second practice is to have one player dominating the court on the short line, the other player feeding high balls onto the front wall from the back of the court which the player at the front must cut off with a volley returning the ball to a length, either straight or cross court. This can be turned into a pressure practice as the defender feeds the ball harder and wider to the front wall, ensuring the attacker has to move more quickly to each ball and be ready earlier for each volley. The roles of the two players are then reversed.

The above practices improve ball control as the forearm muscles (which is where ball control and your strength starts) become stronger and tire less quickly. Once muscles become tired, control is lost.

The Boast

It has already been mentioned that a poor service can be attacked with a volley, however a good service if it doesn't win a rally outright, forces the receiver to play a defensive return off the side wall—known as the boast. As a defensive shot it is usually the last chance a player has of returning the ball, via the side wall to the front wall. However there are two occasions when this shot, played at the back of the court from behind the opponent can be turned into an attacking shot —that is when the opponent is moving backwards from the front of the court to the "T", is on his heels and therefore off balance—or when you know that your opponent is thoroughly exhausted and hasn't the legs to go to the front of the court any more. The defensive shot in these two situations can often be turned into an attacking shot. The forehand boast can be compared with the forehand drive.

Shaping up for the Forehand Boast

(a) Footwork for the Forehand Drive

(b) Footwork for the Forehand Boast

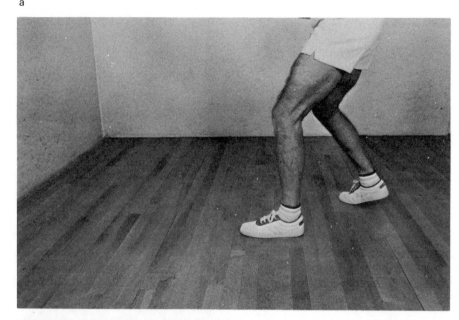

The main difference is in the position of the feet which have to be altered so that instead of the left foot pointing to the side wall, it now points to the corner of the court so that the player's body faces the back wall. The ball is hit up onto the side wall with an identical swing to that for the drive with an open racket face, usually taking the ball slightly in front of the leading left foot at the top of the bounce or just as it falls from the top of the bounce. The weight is transferred on to the front foot with knees and back bent and head well down until the shot has been completed. After

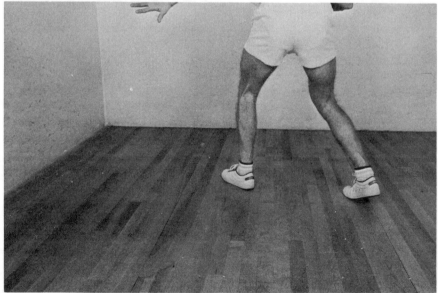

b

60

(a) Backswing
(b) Impact
(c) Follow through
▼

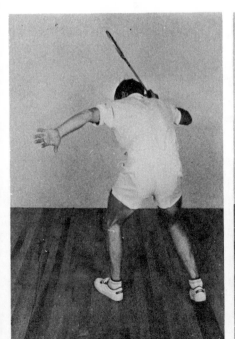

a

b

c

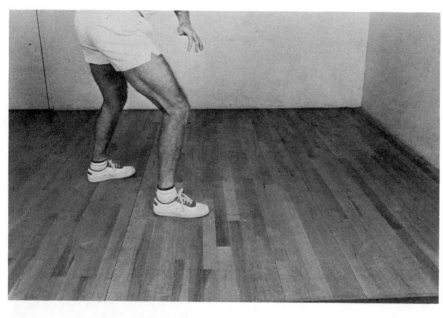

(a) Footwork for the Backhand Drive
(b) Footwork for the Backhand Boast

being hit onto the near side wall the ball should travel across the court to the front wall, dropping into the opposite side wall as near to the floor as possible, and ideally into the nick—the gap where the side wall meets the floor.

Similarly the backhand boast can be compared to the backhand drive, but again with the boast the body faces the back wall with the leading right foot pointing towards the back corner of the court and the shot is hit up on to the near side wall. Concentrate on hitting the ball up with an open racket face onto the side wall correctly, head down until the shot is completed with a good follow through. The ball is hit in front of the right foot.

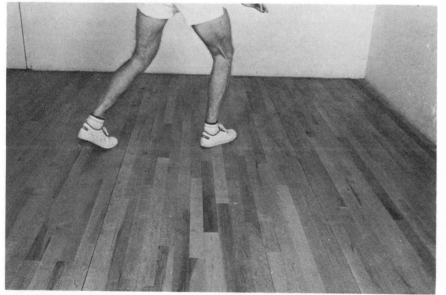

Shaping up for the
Backhand Boast

(a) Backswing
(b) Impact
(c) Follow through

a

b

c

Do not try to drag the ball round to the front wall

On either side do not try and drag the ball round to the front wall—a common mistake on the boast usually resulting in the ball being hit with a closed racket face, and not reaching the front wall. A result with similar consequences will also be given if a player tries to move back to the "T" too soon before the shot has been completed, no weight goes into the shot and the ball doesn't carry to the front wall. There are several teaching aids which will help players who despite correct footwork are still unable to make the ball hit the front wall near the far side wall—instead the ball hits the middle of the front wall ending up in the middle of the court. Firstly if one imagines the ball to reach the top of the bounce directly above the inside corner of the service box, the feet should be placed so that the ball can be hit with an open racket face across the diagonal of the service box hitting the side wall at 45°. Secondly a racket can be placed on the floor to make an angle of 45° with the wall and the racket shaft, the shaft pointing towards the corner that ball is to be played to. Now imagine that the racket shaft is a front wall, and drive the ball up onto that imaginary front wall.

Lastly and perhaps the most effective teaching aid in that it takes the players mind off the front wall (which is the cause of most bad boasts) is to try and hit the ball through the wall into the far front corner of an imaginary adjacent court, hitting the corner at about the height of the cut line. This usually results in a perfect boast, provided the footwork is correct.

Once the shot is completed then move to the "T", eyes on the ball, racket head up, crouched ready for the next shot.

The footwork is important for the boast, particularly when the ball is deep in the corner of the court. It is essential that the leading front foot

is behind the ball. Once the ball has gone behind this foot, which is often the case at the back of the court when the player has not moved far enough into the corner from the "T", then the only way the shot can be played is by flicking the ball back with the wrist. Women have greater difficulty with this technique as they do not always have the strength in their wrists to achieve this.

So remember always get behind the ball to play the shot, especially when it is deep in the corner and give yourself room to hit the ball, don't get too close to it. Keep that racket head well up so that the back wall is not struck by a backswing which has been prepared too late.

It is difficult to practise the boast on one's own, however a good practice in pairs combines alternate drives by one player with alternate forehand and backhand boasts by the other. The player at the front of the court drives the ball to a good

length, keeping the ball out of the wall to help the player boasting. When driving concentrate on good movement to the ball and correct footwork. The player at the back of the court boasts the ball to the opposite front corner of the court so that the drive is then played down the other side wall—and so the practice continues down alternate side walls. Initially in the practice there is cooperation between the players to ensure the practice is beneficial; concentrate on hitting each shot correctly, rather than trying to hit the ball too hard too soon.

The practice can gradually be made more difficult by introducing competition between the players who should try to move back to the "T" after each shot—simulating in practice the game situation. Competition would involve hitting the ball harder and taking the ball earlier but this should only be tried once a good rhythm has been built up—don't compete too soon otherwise the whole purpose of the practice is lost. A back wall boast is another type of boast which can be played in a defensive situation. Although probably a little difficult for the beginner to try it is worth mentioning should you be watching a match in which a more experienced player plays this shot. It is a shot played onto the back wall so that the ball rebounds onto the front wall before bouncing on the floor. The ball must be hit softly up onto the back wall, otherwise there is little chance of it reaching the front wall. It may be played as a forehand or backhand shot. It is important when playing the shot to make sure the ball is hit **up** onto the back wall by hitting under the ball with an open racket face. Do not try to hit against the back wall by hitting through the ball. It is basically a bad shot and should only be used as a last resort in getting the ball to the front wall. Obviously any ball which

floats onto the front wall and then bounces in the front of the court is a risky shot—it allows the opponent a lot of time to position himself to play an attacking shot at the front of the court.

Boasts are normally played defensively from the back of the court. A similar stroke played as an attacking shot, usually at the front of the court, is referred to as an angle. The angle to be most effective is played with the opponent at the back of the court and can either be played from the short line or nearer the front corner of the court. The nearer the angle shot is played to the front corner of the court the greater the risk that the ball after hitting the side and front walls will land in the middle of the court, and for this reason the angle should be played sparingly in a match so that its surprise value can be most effective. If the shot is played at the wrong time with the opponent well up the court, or if

the shot has not been disguised well, the ball is in the front of the court asking to be put away. The same can be said of a reverse angle, which is a shot played across a player's body to the far side wall before hitting the front wall.

The volley boast or angle, the combination of a volley and boast, is a most useful shot and can be used as an attacking shot by the more experienced player. Geoff Hunt and John Easter are two players who use this shot to great effect, dominating a rally from the short line, taking the ball early on the volley, then suddenly, with their opponent at the back of the court, they step in and play a volley boast. Boasts and angles are most useful shots adding variety to your play.

The Forehand Boast

The Dropshot

The dropshot is an attacking shot played at the front of the court and should only be played when the player is balanced and when the opponent is deep in the court. It is often played as a reply to the boast. However the dropshot may also be played from deeper in the court provided the opponent is caught behind the striker, but more accuracy is required as the margin of error is greater.

The forehand dropshot is usually played in the front right half of the court. Start the shot with a good backswing and the racket head well up, not only for early preparation but also for deception. As the ball bounces angle the feet in such a way that a line drawn between the two toes is the line that you want the ball to follow. The ball is hit softly at the top of the bounce, guiding it with an open faced racket onto the front wall so that it drops into the side wall as near to the

c

Forehand Dropshot
(a) Backswing
(b) Impact
(c) Follow through

(a) Backswing
(b) Impact
(c) Follow through

c

floor as possible. A positive follow through ensures that the ball will carry to the front wall.

Bend both knees and back, using the left arm for balance. To ensure the weight is transferred into the shot try to stride to the ball—a long stride will also allow you to move off the ball after your shot is completed more easily. The racket head should be level with the wrist when the ball is struck. The ball should be hit from just in front of the leading foot.

The backhand dropshot is similar, angle the feet so that this time the ball is struck in front of the right foot (for the forehand it was the left foot), guiding the ball at the top of the bounce with an open racket face towards the front wall and into the side wall. Again the player should stride to the shot, but is stationary, with knees and back bent to ensure all the weight is on the leading right foot when the ball is struck.

Remember the dropshot is a delicate shot.

Common errors on the dropshot are that players tend to stand square on to the front wall instead of angling their feet so that the shot can be played to the corner. Do not drop the racket head, often occurring when a player does not stride to the shot but remains too upright. The player usually pushes or pokes at the ball with little, if any,

Backhand Dropshot
(a) Backswing
(b) Impact
(c) Follow through

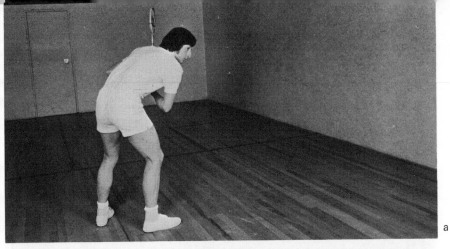

a

b

Backhand Dropshot
(a) Backswing
(b) Impact
(c) Follow through

c

71

Hiscoe plays a Forehand Dropshot from
the middle of the court, with his opponent
Jonah Barrington at the back of the court

Backhand Dropshot:
(A) Straight
(B) Cross Court

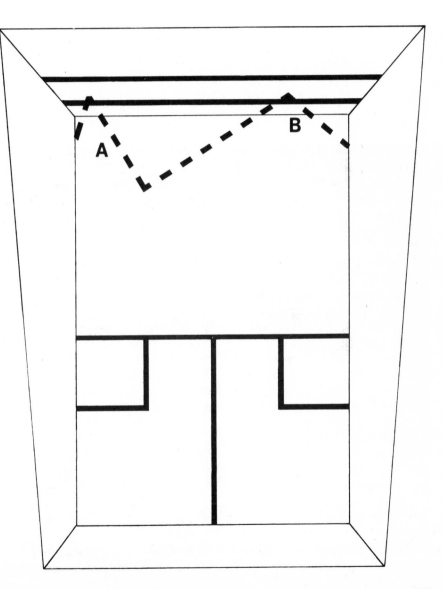

follow through resulting in the ball falling short of the front wall. The straight dropshot is the simplest and most effective dropshot. It has less distance to travel to the front wall than a cross court dropshot and therefore gives the opponent less time to reach the ball. But perhaps more important still if the dropshot is played badly, ie. it is played too high onto the front wall, and is played straight, the chances are that the ball will be somewhere near the side wall making it a difficult return for the opponent. If the ball hits the side wall then it is made even more difficult for the opponent as the ball will be coming at the opponent as he tries to play it. If a cross court dropshot is played badly the ball will end up in the middle of the court and is likely to be killed by the opponent. If you wish to play a cross court dropshot for variation, whether it is played on the forehand or the backhand, do try and play the ball so that after hitting the front wall the ball falls into the far side wall as near to the floor as possible. Use the cross court shot as a variation with discretion for most effect.

One practice for the dropshot is to stand on the "T", feed the ball yourself onto the front wall softly so that you have to move to the ball with good footwork before playing a dropshot to the appropriate corner. Repeat the practice until you are confident that you can hit the side wall, and preferably the nick without having to think about the shot. If you can do this you will find that the shot also becomes automatic in the game and through your practice you will have confidence to play the dropshot (at the right time) in the game. It is one of the most useful shots for moving your opponent into the front corners of the court, and there is nothing more tiring than to be continually put there.

A word about the dropshot played from behind your opponent. This is a risky shot unless your opponent has his eyes glued onto the front wall and does not watch you play the shot or he is too tired to fetch your dropshot. It is risky because your opponent is in front of you and if he reaches your dropshot you are in a defensive position, having played the shot from the back of the court while your opponent is in a most useful attacking position. As an occasional surprise shot it can sometimes be most effective but use it sparingly otherwise you will put yourself in trouble with a dropshot played from behind your opponent. Remember that the dropshot should be played at the front of the court when the striker is balanced and the opponent is deep in the court. A useful combination shot—the volley drop in which the volley is played from around the short line and the ball drops into one of the two front corners of the court. When played with the opponent in the back of the court it is an almost impossible shot to retrieve but in the same breath one should say it is a very difficult shot to perfect and takes a lot of hard practice.

The Dropshot is an attacking shot played
at the front of the court when the player is
balanced with the opponent at the back of
the court

The Lob

The lob is one of the most underrated shots in the game and should be used a lot more than it is, for although it is usually played as a defensive shot, a good lob can often be turned into an attacking shot. Few players use it as an attacking shot in its own right.

The lob is normally played at the front of the court when the striker is off balance or the opponent is well up the court covering the dropshot. As the name implies the shot is hit up on to the front wall, rather like the lob service, so that the ball after rebounding from the front wall drops into the back corners of the court from a height.

Hit up through the ball with an open racket face; keeping the weight into the shot and using a good follow through, even when off balance, will ensure height which prevents the opponent from cutting the ball off and might even force him into a defensive return from the

a

b

c

a

b

c

The Backhand Lob

back of the court. In any event it will have given the striker who was in trouble at the front of the court time to recover, and possibly to get back to the "T".

It is better to hit the ball softly but remember height is the important feature of the lob.

The attacking lob, when hit high and softly, can be played from any part of the court and has several advantages other than putting your opponent in the back of the court. A player has far better ball control and hence accuracy when hitting the ball softly than when hitting it hard; the striker also saves energy so the lob can be used not only to recover during a long rally, but also to vary the pace of a rally and lastly, because there is little pace in the ball, it means the opponent has to make a greater effort if he wishes to raise the pace with his next shot; therefore you are making your opponent do a little more work, which at the end of a long match can take its toll. The lob is more effective played across the court provided it is played high and wide; a shot which is too low and in the middle of the court is asking for trouble. The margin for error is reduced on a cross court lob because of the angles involved. It is not difficult to appreciate that a straight lob can easily be pushed out of above the near side wall because the angles are very narrow. A good cross court lob will often result in an outright winner, particularly on a cold court where the ball dies more easily. Aim to hit the far side wall, after rebounding from the front wall just below the out of court line towards the back of the court, and behind the service box. By hitting the side wall pace is taken off the ball and it will die more quickly. Practice of the lob, and the dropshot for that matter, is difficult on one's own although one can stand on the "T" and feed balls off the front wall to the front corners of the court for practice of each shot. It is a static practice but in the early stages of playing the shot at least it allows one a feel of the shot. One can concentrate on all the main points of the shot and can perfect them until it becomes so automatic that even in a game, a shot from that position can be played correctly without having to think about it. Lobs are usually combined with another shot and are practised in pairs. It might be a forehand lob across court with a backhand boast, so that the practice is across one diagonal of the court. Alternatively it might be a practice combining alternate boasts at the back of the court with alternate lobs from the front, either straight or cross court, or it could even be straight lobs down one side wall with the player at the back of the court feeding short balls to the front of the court. Remember a lob can be used as a defensive or attacking shot, driving the opponent into the back of the court.

Variations of the Basic Shots

So far the basic shots have been discussed, how and when to play them. Obviously there are variations to many shots and combinations (volleyboast, volley dropshot, etc), also alternate shots are possible in a certain situation depending on where the opponent is in relation to the striker. However I have deliberately reduced the number of possibilities to cover the simplest situations. I have done this for one main reason. In watching club players it has become obvious that they always try to play the most complicated shot, probably to fool their opponent but in the end they only place themselves at a dis-advantage.

The simple, safe shots which have been discussed are usually the most effective. Although they don't look spectacular they produce winning squash.

Once the basics have been learnt then the variations may be introduced but only then. Most players learn their squash the other way, putting the cart before the horse, and even better players have to be reminded of the basics from time to time. However, for the beginner, to show that there are usually several possible shots which can be played in any particular situation, consider the example of a ball in the front right quarter of the court, the striker is on balance near the "T" and the opponent, who has just played a backhand boast, is still fairly deep in the court. The striker approaches the shot with the racket head well up and good footwork—the opponent is approaching the "T" but at this stage cannot anticipate the shot. The simple shot would be the straight forehand dropshot, but from the same approach and position the striker could play a cross court dropshot, an angle, a

reverse angle or a straight kill. A kill is a similar shot to the dropshot, the difference being that the ball is hit much harder with a flat racket face but the angles of the shot are the same.

The variations to the straight dropshot should be used sparingly for most effect, for once the angles are read by the opponent the striker is in trouble. It is obvious from the diagram that the angle shots usually end up in the middle of the court and once the opponent has anticipated the shot the striker will be stranded and in a hopeless position.

The straight dropshot has another advantage in that if the shot is played badly, ie. too high onto the front wall, but is played straight, there is a chance it will be some-where near the side wall which makes the opponent's shot more difficult. However a cross court dropshot when played badly will probably be sitting up in the middle

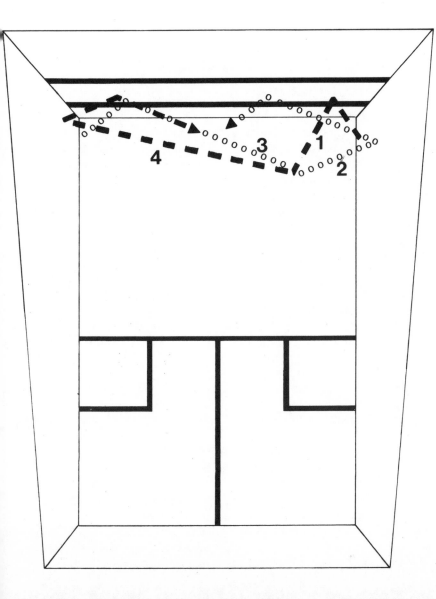

of the court at the front. This is yet another reason why the simple basic shot is often the most effective, although it may not be so exciting to watch or to play—but it will produce winning squash.

Alternative shots from the front of the court showing:
(1) The Forehand Straight Dropshot or Kill
(2) The Angle
(3) The Cross Court Dropshot
(4) The Reverse Angle

Match Play

The Knock-up

Having discussed the shots, how and when to play them, we are now ready to play a match, but before the match starts there is a knock-up. To the foolish players, the knock-up is just a matter of getting the ball warm, but others are learning throughout the five minutes of the knock-up. They are watching, analysing, moving and ensuring their own shots are functioning. Play all your shots during the knock-up correctly, and don't forget your length shots. Don't worry about trying to hide shots from your opponent (if you have any!?)—it is far better to go for them when errors cost nothing than to play a particular shot for the first time in the game and hit it down. At the same time watch for your opponent's weaknesses and strengths, if you don't already know them. Put a few lobs in the air—can he volley? has he played any boasts? or, does he never use the

side wall?—if he doesn't in the knock-up it may well be that he won't in a game except when he is forced to. Has he played any dropshots?—if he hasn't perhaps he can't—in which case he won't give you too much trouble at the front of the court. Always be prepared to adapt your game so that you can play on to your opponent's weaknesses and away from his strengths. Does he look fit? (don't go on what he told you in the changing room) or has he a beer pot, in which case the longer you can keep the rallies going the less trouble he is likely to give you as the game progresses. If he is tall, he won't like low balls and he will probably be slow turning so boast and dropshots could put him in trouble. But he will have a long reach so will probably volley well; take care with those high shots. Conversely the small, wiry player might be fast round the court but won't be able to reach a few good lobs. One realises pretty quickly that

on court it's not the "friendly" game you once thought!—as soon as the match starts you are trying to make it as hard and as difficult as you can for your poor opponent, and of course to be able to do that you must have a game which can be adapted—and this is where all the hours of practice on your shots now comes into its own.
Not only will the condition of your opponents vary, so too will the courts. Apart from the dimensions of the court which are standard, unfortunately no two courts are alike and your play might have to adapt to the court—low or high ceilings, poor background lighting, dark roof, slow or fast walls and floors. Remember, always turn a disadvantage into an advantage. A word of warning here about sweating courts. You might have the misfortune to play on a court when, due to abnormal atmospheric conditions, condensation starts to form on the walls which then

become wet. This means that you virtually have to cut out any side wall shots—otherwise the ball skids off the wet wall and usually goes straight into the roof—out of court. You are restricted to straight or cross court shots so rely on winners only from a good length, perfect width or a winning dropshot. Even lobs will have to be cut out of your game as the lob tends to skid off the front wall into the roof.

Before discussing the Basic Tactics in match play, there are several important general points which must be discussed and should be remembered throughout any match.

Eye on the Ball

Probably the most important and perhaps obvious comment is to make sure that you always keep your eye on the ball. By telling a player to hit the ball at a particular position—ie. at the top of the bounce—you do in fact, indirectly, tell a player to watch the ball. Most players are watching the ball when they hit it themselves. The troubie starts when a player hits the ball behind him to the opponent at the back of the court. Most players then keep their eyes glued to the front wall waiting for the ball to appear. They have no idea where the ball is going or what shot their opponent has played. If a shot is played to the front corner of the court by the time the ball is in their line of vision it is usually too late to do much about it. Only by watching the ball all the time can a player see whether his opponent is about to play a hard or soft shot, a boast or a straight drive, thereby allowing

How not to stand on the 'T'—racket head dangling, eyes glued to the front wall

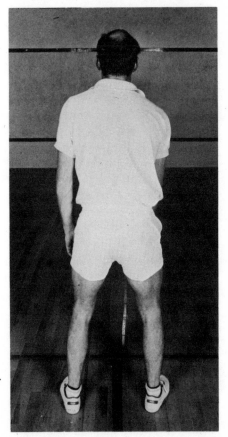

some measure of anticipation for the return shot. So when you do manage to dominate the court from the central "T" position **watch the ball,** especially when it goes behind you.

The correct position on the 'T'. Eye on the ball, racket head well up, crouched ready to move to the next shot

Racket Head Up

Earlier in the book we discussed the importance of keeping your racket head well up in the preparation of each shot. It is not a bad idea to remind you all again that during a rally you must still keep that racket head up.
It will allow you

    (a) early preparation of your shot

    (b) the opportunity to wrong foot your opponent by delaying the shot

    (c) to go deeper into the back of the court

    (d) the chance to kill the ball at the front of the court by hitting the ball down into the nick.

So do make a habit of keeping that **racket head up** throughout the rally—keeping the wrist cocked ensuring a right angle between the vertical racket shaft and the forearm. There are far too many players who move about the court with the racket head dangling down near the floor—the surest way to a loose wrist and a hasty backswing which

Geoff Hunt demonstrates a racket head well up

Geoff Hunt and Gogi Alauddin, Semi-Final
British Open Championship 1973. Hunt,
moves in to play a Forehand, racket head
up and perfectly balanced

Again the familiar pose of Hunt, moving
in to play another Forehand Drive against
Alauddin

leads to those snatched uncontrolled shots.

Movement on Court

The sign of a good player is one who appears to have all the time in the world to play a shot. He appears to glide round the court making each shot look effortless. The secret of his success to a large extent is in his movement to the ball—he is always perfectly balanced and stationary when hitting the ball. The answer, when analysed, is that he has used a long (last) stride to the ball. His feet are well apart which means his body is low, with knees and back bent with all his weight on that leading foot. With weight on the leading foot and feet astride the player is balanced to play the shot. He is also in a position which enables him to push back to the "T" off the leading foot, ensuring that he moves back from the ball to allow his opponent a fair view of the ball and freedom of his stroke on the next shot.

Most beginners tend to run to the ball, arriving at the shot with feet close together in an upright position. In this stance there is little weight on the front foot, and if the ball is low the tendency is to drop the racket head to meet the ball. On striking the ball it is too easy to either pull away from the shot too soon, run through the shot as the ball is hit or pivot on one foot with a resultant swivelling of the body which usually produces a bad shot.

Movement back to the "T" is also a problem as there is little chance of pushing back, instead a player starts to run back often having turned to run forwards to the "T" with his back to the front wall. The correct movement is to stride backwards towards the "T", with the body still facing the front wall. Movement between shots should be as economical as possible with as few steps before the final long stride to the ball. Always try to be on your toes so that you can move

Geoff Hunt moves to the ball on the
backhand, demonstrating beautifully the
principle of getting your racket head up
for the shot

in any direction quickly—if you are caught on your heels you become flatfooted and will struggle to reach a ball in the corners of the court. A crouching, rather than upright position, will help that initial pounce towards the ball. So the correct position on the "T" will be a player on his toes, crouched ready to move to any corner of the court, eye following the ball, with the racket head well up. Not the cocktail party stance, straight back, legs stiff, eyes glazed on the front wall, racket head dangling down near the floor. Learn to adopt the correct position and in just one long stride you will be amazed how much of the court you can cover.

Correct position on the 'T'   ▶

Basic Tactics

The "T" is the central position in the squash court and therefore it is logical that from that position you have the least distance to travel to any of the four corners of the court. It is the dominant position from which the battle is commanded and therefore it is your aim to try to get back to the "T" after each shot, and to keep your opponent off it. To do this you must keep the ball out of the middle of the court and for the first time you can now realise how important it is to develop the straight length drive down the walls. The ball can then be kept out of the middle of the court and so consequently your opponent will be prevented from taking up a position on the "T". It can also be realised how a bad cross court shot would enable your opponent, if he was already on the "T" when the cross court shot was played, to cut the ball off as it passed close to the "T". However, a well judged cross court shot not only takes your

Dominating the 'T'

opponent from the "T", it prevents him cutting the ball off with a volley and takes him to the back of the court to play a difficult shot as the ball, having hit the side wall, comes in at him.

Domination of the "T" is the first basic tactic in the game of squash. Having learned to dominate the "T", the question now asked is where should I keep my opponent? Provided your opponent is off the "T" it will mean that he is playing his shots near or in one of the four corners and he will be doing most of the running and should therefore be tiring first. Initially to dominate the rally it is important to keep your opponent on the defensive that is at the back of the court. We are back to our basic shots—the length drives. Only if you have perfected a length drive will you be able to keep your opponent in the back corners of the court. If you have him stuck at the back there is little he should do in such a defensive

position other than to play a defensive shot; there is little chance of him hitting a winning shot from the back of the court provided you are watching the ball. Also the margin for error is far greater from the back of the court so if he does go for that desperate winner the chances are that he will hit the tin, especially when he starts to tire. Therefore by keeping your opponent at the back of the court it won't be too long before he is forced to play the ball into the front half of the court. When that happens you are balanced, having dominated the "T", to move forward to play an attacking shot—maybe an outright winner.

Most winning shots do come from the front of the court, so you are trying to create this winning position for yourself. If you analyse nearly all games within a squash match it is the player who has remained in the front of the court who wins the game.

Most winning shots come from the front of the court

Having created a winning position, be positive and go for your shot—whether it's your first shot, or the twenty-first or the hundred and twenty-first shot in the rally. Don't just keep the rally going with length drives for the sake of it, when you have the opportunity to attack do so. By playing a shot to the front of the court you will start to move your opponent forward. Movement up and down the court is very tiring—far more so than just moving from side to side—especially when stretching for dropshots and reaching for lobs. So many players having created an attacking position at the front of the court, instead of playing the ball short to move the opponent up the court, just thump the ball to the back of the court, without thinking, straight back to the opponent who hasn't had to move at all.

It can be seen that the basic shots in a rally are ones of length to keep the opponent at the back of the court in a defensive position. From that position he will eventually play the ball to the front of the court where you will now be in a position to play an attacking shot—usually the dropshot or angle—both shots being most useful to drag the opponent into the front of the court. Once the enemy is moved up and down the court, he will start to tire and a tiring opponent is usually a beaten opponent. Of course there will be many occasions when you will find yourself in the back of the court as the opponent—then you must play a safe defensive shot to try and restore your position on the "T". Play the ball back down the wall, to a length, to bring your dominating opponent to the back of the court. Or a high wide cross court shot will have the same effect if he is anticipating a straight shot. When in the back of the court don't try to hit the ball as hard and low as possible—it will not get you out of trouble but may put you further in

it—if the ball doesn't actually hit the tin, it will be bouncing in the front of the court and is inviting your opponent into an attacking position. One must not only have the patience but also the fitness to be able to manoeuvre yourself into this attacking or possibly winning position. Don't go for your winners too soon in the rally, it normally has sad consequences, bide your time and your position will come.

Think on Court

While applying these basic tactics in the course of a match it is essential that you are always thinking on the court. You must always be aware of your opponent's position, for this should influence your next shot. So many players hit the ball straight back to their opponent whereas with a little thought they could have placed the ball at the furthest corner away from him. Always think positively, so that when you have created an attacking position for yourself, make use of it.

If you are thinking on court you will realise that you can go for your shots more freely as hand in or server, for a rally lost only means losing the service. However a rally lost as hand out means a point to the opponent hence it is more important to make sure that your winning shots are really 'on' as hand out. You should not be battering the tin when hand out!!

More care should be taken too as each game nears its conclusion. A stupid shot or careless mistake early in the game is not nearly so vital as a silly point lost near the end of the game—it is easier to catch up on points when only a few have been scored but from six onwards it may well be too late. So if you watch good players in a match—and this is one of the best ways of learning to play—it will explain why rallies tend to become longer as the game proceeds, players cannot afford to make errors and only go for the winner when a good opportunity is presented, otherwise a safe defensive shot is preferred. But even at this stage in the game it is still important to think positively and look for ways of creating the opening for an attacking shot or winner—a lost opportunity can often mean the difference between winning or losing the game.

Match Tactics

Having lost a game it is important that you should know why you have lost it—another reason for thinking on court. You will have to adapt your game and this change in play brings the reader into the realms of Match Tactics.

The difference between Basic and Match Tactics is that Basic Tactics should be applied throughout each game in every match. Match Tactics however vary over a match depending on the court, the opponent and how each game is going. For example never change a winning game—but if you have lost a game you will have to do something about it! It may be that you are hitting all your dropshots into the tin so you must either cut that shot out for the time being or better still play the shot more safely by hitting the ball a little higher onto the front wall. Your opponent conversely might be hitting a particular shot which is winning him a lot of points—if so, do you know

which shot it is? In the next game he should not be given more chances to play this winning shot; if you do then you are asking for trouble. Match Tactics therefore are concerned with your ability to read a game. Reading the game is an advanced technique and will be difficult for inexperienced players to understand but it is important to encourage all players at whatever level to do it. You can practise your reading of the game in the gallery when you watch a match. It is often a lot easier to see what is happening from the gallery than it is when you are actually on the court playing. Do the players play a hard and fast or a slow controlled game? Where are the winners coming from? What are the players weaknesses? Do they anticipate the opponents shot quickly? Concentrate on the players' movement, are they being moved into the corners of the court? Teach yourself good thinking habits in the gallery.

Conditioned Games

It is difficult to teach players to think on court. However there are several conditioned games which can be played which not only make the players practise a particular tactic in the game situation, but also help them to concentrate, discipline their game and think—all essential requirements of good squash playing.

For instance players who are having trouble hitting the ball to a length, play a normal game but lose a rally every time the ball bounces in front of the short line. This is particularly good practice for players who, without thinking, continually play the ball into the front of the court—a common error made by beginners (and many club players). If a player loses a point when the ball does bounce in the front of the court, then of course both players are trying to force their opponent to boast from the back of the court. It is very difficult to play this shot so that the ball does not land in the front of the court thereby presenting the opponent with an easy attacking shot—and this is just what you are trying to achieve in a normal game. Once the opponent is forced to boast you have created an attacking situation and possibly a winning position. This conditioned game assumes you can hit an outright winner at the front of the court.

A similar restriction could be applied in practice if one player is considerably better than his opponent. Their game can be made more even if the better player is restricted to playing the ball to a length while the weaker opponent plays a normal game. Players who hit too many cross court shots can use a conditioned game to make them play the ball straight. This is best done when one player plays a normal game while the opponent can only play the ball straight. This means that he has to cut out all cross court shots, boasts and angles, and will only hit a winning shot with a good straight dropshot, a perfect length or a shot which is so tight against the side wall that his opponent hits the wall and misses the ball.

Players who never volley, but leave everything to go to the back wall, can be made to take the ball earlier if they lose a rally every time the ball hits the back wall. This conditioned game teaches players to apply pressure to their opponent which can be done either by taking the ball earlier (i.e. volleying), hitting the ball harder or a combination of the two. But beginners should remember that if the ball is hit harder, some control is lost.

Having learnt to think, concentrate and discipline your game. It is important that these requirements are maintained throughout a match. Squash, however, is an energetic game and as players chase the little black ball round the court they tend to tire, some sooner than others. As soon as players tire physically, mental tiredness sets in also and not only is concentration lost but players stop thinking and any discipline (if there was any in the first place) is gone. To maintain mental alertness and to be able to reach the ball at the end of a long match one has to be fit.

Fitness Training

Squash is a game of skill, speed and fitness. However all the skill in the world will not enable you to hit the ball if you can't reach it. So despite the claims of most players who play squash to keep fit, if you really want to improve your game (other than by improving your ball control) you will need to get fit.

Few books on squash give any details on how to train for squash. Most players up to a few years ago just went on the court and played matches—that was their training. However in 1966 Jonah Barrington became the first British player to win the Open for 28 years, and his win, based on supreme physical fitness backed up by tremendous discipline, revolutionised our ideas on fitness training for squash. His philosophy has been proved again when Bryan Patterson reached the final of the International Individual Championship, only the second British player to do so since its inauguration in 1967, largely because of his attitude and dedication towards training for squash.

Any training schedule for squash must be geared to the season, by that I mean training out of season should be aimed at building up stamina in preparation for the forthcoming season. Stamina is the basis of all fitness. Training might take the form of long distance running—a soul destroying occupation for some—weight training for those with access to a gymnasium and a good instructor who can gear schedules directly to squash needs, exercises similarly designed, and skipping. Of these running is probably the best, forming a solid foundation as a basis on which other forms of training can be geared.

As the season approaches the long distance running for stamina would be changed to fartlek or interval running so that the short sharp bursts which are required in squash are slowly introduced. Weights would be reduced but bursts of high activity with high repetitions would be increased. During the season training sessions have to be reduced because of the matches which are being played, and it is very much a matter of trial and error discovering how much training can be fitted into match schedules. Don't tire yourself so much in training that you are too exhausted to play—each time you step onto a court you should be raring to go—so training should be kept ticking over but that's all.

Of course I am now writing for the match player, but even beginners can help to improve their game if they become fitter, and for those who have little time to train or who prefer to play I outline two schedules which would take very little of your time and yet if done twice a week regularly would improve your fitness and hence your game beyond your wildest dreams. Firstly a few exercises to strengthen the muscles used in squash. It is important to go through the full range of movement each time in each exercise. You are not helping yourself if you cheat!

1. Punch Ups, running on the spot
   —This is running on the spot making sure your knees come up high so that your feet are at least 12 inches off the ground. Keep your legs firm and do not allow yourself to wobble all over the place. Simultaneously, you must do punch ups. Tuck your elbows in close to your waist and punch straight up, fist clenched, until your arm is fully extended. As your right leg comes up, so you punch with your left arm. Similarly, with the left leg and right arm. Repetitions counted with each right arm punch.

2. Press Ups—Front support position on toes and palms with hands shoulder width apart and body straight. Bend arms (not body) so that the side of your face just touches the floor, and straighten arms—do not allow your body to touch the floor— repeat.

3. Leg Wobbles—Lie flat on back, clasping hands behind neck. Raise head 6 inches off ground and raise both heels off the ground—half an inch to an inch —and slowly wobble feet up and down, 9 to 10 inches alternately. Keep your legs straight and stiffened. Do not bend your knees. Repetitions counted for each right leg wobble.

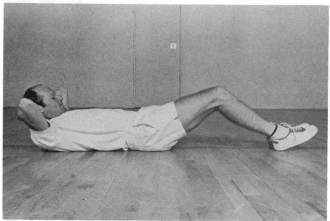

4. Sit Ups—Sit on floor, legs
together extended in front,
hands clasped behind your neck.
Lie back on the floor, then come
up bending forward to place
your head on the right side of
your knees, to the centre and the
left, before lying back again.

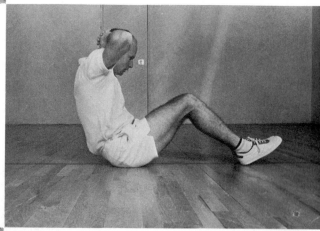

5. Knees to Chest—With your arms outstretched sideways, jump up, bringing your knees up to your chest. After each knees-to-chest, do a small balancing jump, and then up again—high and low alternate jumps.

6. Skipping—Use a good heavy rope and vary the steps but always try to land as lightly as possible. Rate of work should be 100 steps per minute. Count number of times that you falter during the time and record.

The Test Rate
Before starting the exercise schedule determine your own Test Rate by doing as many repetitions of each exercise in circuit 1 for one minute—or until you can do no more. Allow one minute rest between each exercise. This is your Test Rate.

The Training Rate
Your Training Rate is half the Test Rate.

A Circuit

Do each exercise once at the Training Rate. Repeat the circuit three times, repeating the exercises in the same order each time. Allow a minute rest between each circuit, but not between each exercise. Record the time taken to do the three circuits.

Always warm up for five minutes before you start any form of training. The training is not an end in itself but is designed to help you play better squash, and is never a substitute for practice. However squash is a fast game and as competition becomes fiercer only the fittest players will survive. You need to be fit to reach the ball; if you are unable to reach the ball all the skill in the world will not enable you to hit it. At the end of every second week repeat the Test Rate, you will be surprised how you have improved on your original rate.

Court Training

The exercises can be done anywhere, but perhaps the best form of training for squash should be on a squash court and probably the hardest training schedule is a form of circuit training devised by Jonah Barrington on a squash court, which he calls court training.

Court training is done without a ball so that correct movement and footwork about the court is the only requirement the player needs to concentrate on. There is no ball or opponent to have to worry about. Start on the "T" in the correct position of readiness, then move quickly to any corner using long

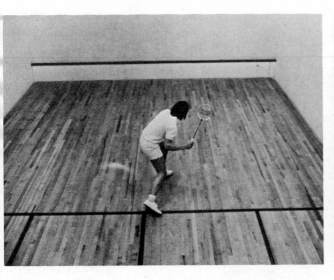

strides into a position where an imaginary shot is played correctly—knees bent, body low over the ball with a good swing of the racket and correct footwork. Do not remain upright, with feet close together with a prod for a shot. Then move back to the "T", with a good push back initially off that leading foot. If the movement to the corner was poor or the footwork when playing the shot was bad, then for your next movement from the "T" go back to the same corner and if necessary continue going to the corner until the movement and footwork is correct.

From the "T" go to each corner

◄ Move to all corners

concentrating on good movement and footwork, keeping that racket head well up. Play a full imaginary shot and back to the "T". Continue the movements for half a minute then have a recovery period which can vary. To start with, the recovery period will probably be considerably longer than your working period, but as your fitness improves cut down this recovery period until it is the same or less than your working time.

Fitness after all is the ability to recover. Everyone tires in squash, the difference between the fitter players is that they recover more quickly, while those who are not fit never recover at all ! !

Obviously the pace at which you move round the court can vary so to be working well you should try to go into at least 12 corners (ie. 12 movements) in your half minute work period. Gradually increase the number of work sessions you can do, and in this way you will improve your fitness. The optimum training schedule would be a 10 session work-out geared to time periods of 40 seconds on and 10 to 15 seconds off. This ties in nicely with the average lengths of rallies and rest periods in the course of a normal match. It would only take 10 minutes to complete and therefore there is no excuse on the grounds of "not enough time" for not doing such a schedule at least twice a week!!

But a word of warning—this **is** a **very** hard form of training and it is extremely tiring, as anyone who tries it will discover. Build up slowly, as with any training schedule, don't go mad to start with. If you can train, do so regularly rather than having one long session irregularly—this does very little good in the long run. It's the slow accumulation over a long period of time which pays dividends. Do any court training as your last schedule—if you are not fit you

would be very unwise to try and play after it—your leg muscles become tired and if you play at the end of a court training session you will pull one of those tiring muscles. Even five minutes court training three times a week would make a world of difference to your fitness. Always try to work in pairs—the competition and personal pride will push you harder than if you were on your own. And it's not a bad idea if you can persuade a time keeper on the gallery to indicate the time periods for you, as well as to shout, encourage and push you into that little extra effort each time. It can be an amusing spectacle for any spectators in the gallery watching a "maniac" rush round the court chasing an imaginary ball—ignore any comments or mirth and as you stagger off the court gasping for air you will come off knowing that the last laugh will be on them when in a few weeks you can run them into the ground. It's

the training for squash on and off court which should be hard—if it's done properly the game should be easy.

Rules Refereeing and Marking

While I do not intend this last chapter to be a repetition of the rules it is important that even the beginner should understand one or two basic rules and at the same time it will serve as a useful reminder to the better players, some of whom think they know the rules, others who still have no idea. Having discussed a match it is logical to mention that there are two officials who will be in the gallery controlling the match. The officials are known as the Marker and the Referee.

The Marker
The Marker controls the game by calling the score and makes sure that the points are won correctly. He introduces the match and the players and during the course of play indicates if the ball has gone out of court, bounced twice or hits the tin. He also calls the faults on service which have already been discussed. To ensure that the score is correct and that the players serve from the correct boxes he will write the score down. He will also repeat any decision that the referee might have to make before calling the score.

The Referee
The referee is in overall charge of the match and is there to ensure a correct and fair outcome to each rally. He is the official to whom any appeal is made by either player if they think that the marker has made a mistake in calling or if there has been some form of interference during a rally. Having answered an appeal, his decision is final. He must keep a check on the marker and for that reason should also write down the score. The referee is responsible for the rules regarding time—the knock up of 5 minutes; while the interval between games is one minute and between the fourth and fifth it is two minutes.

If only one official is available he must first assume the role of the marker, then when required he acts as a referee.

Hitting an Opponent with the Ball

With two players in an enclosed space and with the ball travelling around the court fast and in various directions there will be occasions when a player is unfortunately struck with the ball. To avoid queries by players and particularly beginners to the game let's discuss the outcome of various situations which might occur during a rally.

If the striker hits his opponent with the ball which otherwise would have gone directly to the front wall as a good return, that is above the tin, then the striker wins the rally, and if he was the server he scores a point. The reason for this decision is that the opponent has obstructed the striker's shot or ability to play the ball to any part of the front wall to which he is entitled, so the striker rightly wins the rally.

However there are two exceptions to this rule, which would only result in a let ball, in other words the rally would be restarted and played again. Firstly, if the striker has before striking the ball, turned on the ball before playing it, in other words followed the ball round and then having hit it strikes the opponent it is only a let. 'Turning' can occur anywhere on the court but normally is in one of the back corners of the court. It is potentially a dangerous situation and as a let can be the only outcome if the opponent is hit it would be far better to refrain from hitting the ball and play a let anyway.

Secondly if a player has already attempted a shot (probably a volley) but misses the ball and then on the second attempt hits the opponent with the ball, that too would only be a let.

Lastly if the striker hits the opponent but the ball was going to the side wall before hitting the front wall then a let is played. Likewise if the ball having hit a side wall then hits the opponent on its way to the front wall that too is a let.

If the striker's shot would not have hit the front wall above the tin then the opponent would win the rally.

Freedom of Stroke

The other situation which normally occurs accidentally with beginners on court but can be caused deliberately by better players, concerns the actual playing of a shot. Having played a stroke the player must now make every effort to get out of the way to allow his opponent to move directly to the ball and to play at the ball. The opponent as well as having this freedom of stroke is also entitled to a fair view of the ball, in other words he should be able to see the ball, be able to reach it to play it, and finally he is allowed to hit the ball to any part of the front wall.

As a general rule then try and play the ball away from yourself then these problems which are referred to in Rule 17 can often be avoided. If the ball accidentally goes down the middle of the court then it is up to the striker to keep out of the middle of the court, hence the "T", to allow his opponent to hit the ball.

If interference occurs and on appeal in the opinion of the referee a player has not made every effort to move away the rally is awarded to the obstructed player. In other words the player has stood on his shot which is classed as a case of deliberate obstruction.

In the case of accidental obstruction, when one player does move away after the stroke but moves in the wrong direction causing a collision, and the referee thinks that his opponent was prevented from playing a winning shot, the rally is awarded to the opponent.

However if in the case of accidental obstruction the obstructed player could have only played the ball, but could not have played a winning shot, then the decision on appeal is a let.

If the obstructed player could not have reached the ball, then the player who has just played the ball wins the rally.

Most collisions occur when a player plays the ball back into the same quarter of the court in which he has just played the shot. To avoid obstruction the player should then move in an arc, moving inwards toward the centre of the court before going back to the "T". Do not move straight back to the "T" as this is the path the incoming striker is entitled to take from the "T" to play the ball.

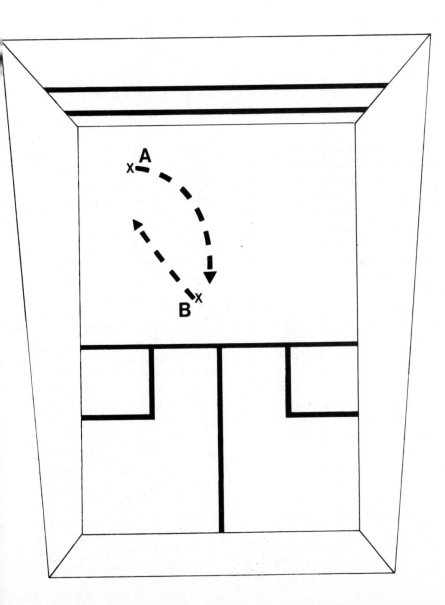

(A) Striker
(B) Incoming player

Diagram shows correct movement of
(A) back to the "T" allowing (B) direct
access to the ball which has been played
to the front of the court by (A) and thus
avoiding a collision.

Rules

The Rules of Squash Rackets

The Singles Game approved by the International Squash Rackets Federation

(Copies of these rules, suitable for framing, can be obtained from the S.R.A. at 70p post free)

1. **The Game, How Played.** The game of squash rackets is played between two players with standard rackets, with balls bearing the standard mark of the S.R.A. and in a rectangular court of standard dimensions enclosed on all four sides. .

2. **The Score.** A match shall consist of the best of three or five games at the option of the promoters of the competition. Each game is 9 up: that is to say the player who first wins 9 points wins the game except that, on the score being called 8-all for the first time, hand-out may, if he chooses, before the next service is delivered, set the game to 10, in which case the player who first scores two more points wins the game. Hand-out must in either case clearly indicate his choice to the marker, if any, and to his opponent.

Note to Referees

If hand-out does not make clear his choice before the next service, the referee shall stop play and require him to do so.

3. **Points, How Scored.** Points can only be scored by hand-in. When a player fails to serve or to make a good return in accordance with the rules, his opponent wins the stroke. When hand-in wins a stroke, he scores a point; when hand-out wins a stroke, he becomes hand-in.

4. **The Right to Serve.** The right to serve first is decided by the spin of a racket. Thereafter the Server continues to serve until he loses a stroke, when his opponent becomes the server, and so on throughout the match.

5. **Service.** The ball before being struck shall be thrown in the air and shall not touch the walls or floor. The ball shall be served on to the front wall so that on its return, unless volleyed, it would fall to the floor in the quarter court nearest the back wall and opposite to the server's box from which the service has been delivered. A player with the use of only one arm may utilize his racket to project the ball into the air.

At the beginning of each game and of each hand, the server may serve from either box, but after scoring a point he shall then serve from the other and so on alternately as long as he remains hand-in or until the end of the game. If the server serves from the wrong box there shall be no penalty and the service shall count as if served from the right box, except that hand-out may, if he does not attempt to take the service, demand that it be served from the other box.

6. **Good Service.** A service is good which is not a fault or which does

not result in the server serving his hand out in accordance with rule 9. If the server serves one fault he shall serve again.

7. Fault. A service is a fault (unless the server serves his hand-out under rule 9):

(a) If the server fails to stand with one foot at least within and not touching the line surrounding the service box (called a foot fault);

(b) If the ball is served on to or below the cut line;

(c) If the ball served first touches the floor on or in front of the short line;

(d) If the ball served first touches the floor in the wrong half court or on the half-court line.

(The wrong half court is the left for a service from the left-hand box and the right for a service from the right-hand box).

8. Fault, if Taken. Hand-out may take a fault. If he attempts to do so, the service thereupon becomes good and the ball continues in play.

If he does not attempt to do so, the ball shall cease to be in play provided that, if the ball, before it has bounced twice upon the floor, touches the server or anything he wears or carries, the server shall lose the stroke.

9. Serving Hand-Out. The server serves his hand-out and loses the stroke:

(a) If the ball is served on to or below the board or out of court or against any part of the court before the front wall;

(b) If he fails to strike the ball or strikes the ball more than once;

(c) If he serves two consecutive faults;

(d) If the ball before it has bounced twice upon the floor, or has been struck by his opponent touches the server or anything he wears or carries.

10. Let. A let is an undecided stroke and the service or rally in respect of which a let is allowed shall not count and the server shall serve

again from the same box. A let shall not annul a previous fault.

11. The Play. After a good service has been delivered the players return the ball alternately until one or other fails to make a good return or the ball otherwise ceases to be in play in accordance with the rules.

12. Good Return. A return is good if the ball, before it has bounced twice upon the floor, is returned by the striker on to the front wall above the board without touching the floor or any part of the striker's body or clothing, provided the ball is not hit twice or out of court.

Note to Referees

It shall not be considered a good return if the ball touches the board either before or after it hits the front wall.

13. Strokes, How Won. A player wins a stroke:

(a) Under rule 9;

(b) If his opponent fails to make a good return of the ball in play;

(c) If the ball in play touches the

striker or his opponent or anything he wears or carries, except as is otherwise provided by rules 14 and 15.

14. **Hitting an Opponent with the Ball.** If an otherwise good return of the ball has been made, but before reaching the front wall it hits the striker's opponent or his racket or anything he wears or carries then:

(a) If the ball would have made a good return and would have struck the front wall without first touching any other wall, the striker shall win the stroke, except that, if the striker shall have followed the ball round and so turned before making a stroke, a let shall be allowed;

(b) If the ball would otherwise have made a good return, a let shall be allowed;

(c) If the ball would not have made a good return, the striker shall lose the stroke.

The ball shall cease to be in play, even if it subsequently goes up.

15. **Further Attempts to Hit the Ball.** If the striker strikes at and misses the ball, he may make further attempts to return it. If after being missed, the ball accidentally touches his opponent or his racket or anything he wears or carries, then:

(a) If the striker could otherwise have made a good return, a let shall be allowed;

(b) If the striker could not have made a good return he loses the stroke.

If any such further attempt is successful but the ball before reaching the front wall hits the striker's opponent or his racket or anything he wears or carries, a let shall be allowed and rule 14 (a) shall not apply.

16. **Appeals.** An appeal may be made against any decision of the marker.

(i) The following rules shall apply to appeals on the service:

(a) No appeal shall be made in respect of foot faults.

(b) No appeal shall be made in respect of the marker's call of "fault" to the first service.

(c) If the marker calls "fault" to the second service, the server may appeal and, if the decision is reversed, a let shall be allowed.

(d) If the marker does not call "fault" or "out of court" to the second service, hand-out may appeal even if he attempts to take the ball, and if the decision is reversed, hand-out becomes hand-in.

(e) If the marker does not call "fault" or "out of court" to the first service, hand-out may appeal if he makes no attempt to take the ball. If the appeal is disallowed, hand-out shall lose the stroke.

(ii) An appeal under rule 12 or 16 (i) (d) shall be made at the end of the rally in which the stroke in dispute has been played.

(iii) In all cases where an appeal for a let is desired, this appeal shall be made by addressing the referee

ith the words, "Let, please". Play
hall thereupon cease until the
»feree has given his decision.

(iv) No appeal may be made after
1e delivery of a service for anything
1at occurred before that service
/as delivered.

7. Fair View and Freedom of
troke.

(a) After making a stroke a player
1ust get out of his opponent's way
s much as possible.

, in the opinion of the referee, a
layer has not made every effort to
o this the referee shall stop play
nd award a stroke to his opponent.

(b) When a player:

(i) fails to give his opponent a
air view of the ball.

Note: a player shall be considered
o have had a fair view unless the
all returns too close to his
»pponent for the player to sight it
dequately for the purpose of
naking a stroke);

(ii) fails to avoid interfering with,
»r crowding his opponent in getting

to or striking at the ball;

(iii) fails to allow his opponent, as
far as his opponent's position allows
him, freedom to play the ball to any
part of the front wall and to either
side wall near the front wall, the
referee may on appeal, or without
waiting for an appeal, allow a let;
but, if in the opinion of the referee, a
player has not made every effort to
comply with these requirements of
the rule, the referee shall stop play
and award a stroke to his opponent.
Notwithstanding anything
contained above, if a player suffers
interference from or distraction by
his opponent, and in the opinion of
the referee, is thus prevented from
making a winning return, he shall be
awarded the stroke.

Note to Referees

(a) The practice of impeding an
opponent's strokes by crowding or
by obscuring his view is highly
detrimental to the game and
referees should have no hesitation
in enforcing the penultimate

paragraph of this rule.

(b) The words "interfering with . . .
his opponent in getting to . . . the
ball" must be interpreted so as to
include the case of a player having
to wait for an excessive swing of his
opponent's racket.

18. **Let, When Allowed.** Notwithstanding anything contained in
these rules:

(i) A let may be allowed:

(a) If, owing to the position of
the striker, his opponent is unable to
avoid being touched by the ball
before the return is made.

Note to Referees

This rule shall be construed to
include the cases of the striker
whose position in front of his
opponent makes it impossible for
the latter to see the ball or who
shapes as if to play the ball and
changes his mind at the last moment
preferring to take the ball off the
back wall, the ball in either case
hitting the opponent, who is
between the striker and the back

wall. This is not, however, to be taken as conflicting in any way with the referee's duties under rule 17.

(b) If the ball in play touches any article lying in the court;

(c) If the player refrains from hitting the ball owing to a reasonable fear of injuring his opponent;

(d) If the player in the act of striking touches his opponent;

(e) If the referee is asked to decide an appeal and is unable to do so;

(f) If the player drops his racket, calls out or in any other way distracts the attention of his opponent and the referee considers such occurrence to have caused his opponent to lose the stroke.

(ii) A let shall be allowed:

(a) If hand-out is not ready and does not attempt to take the service;

(b) If a ball breaks during play;

(c) If an otherwise good return has been made, but the ball goes out of court on its first bounce;

(d) As provided for by rules 14,

15, 16 (i) (c) and 22.

(iii) Provided always that no let shall be allowed:

(a) In respect of any stroke which a player attempts to make, unless in making the stroke he touches his opponent, except as provided for under rules 18 (ii) (b) and (c) and 15.

(b) Unless the striker could have made a good return.

(iv) Unless an appeal is made by one of the players, no let shall be allowed except where these rules definitely provide for a let, namely rules 14 (a), 14 (b) and 17 and paragraphs (ii) (b) and (c) of rule 18.

19. **New Ball.** At any time when the ball is not in actual play a new ball may be substituted by mutual consent of the players or on appeal by either player at the discretion of the referee.

20. **Knock-up.** The referee shall allow to either player or to the two players together a period of five

minutes during the hour preceding the start of a match for knocking up in a court in which a match is to be played. The choice of knocking-up first shall be decided by the spin of a racket.

21. **Play in a Match is to be Continuous.** After the first service is delivered, play shall be continuous so far as is practical, provided that at any time play may be suspended owing to bad light or other circumstances beyond the control of the players for such period as the referee shall decide. The referee shall award the match to the opponent of any player who, in his opinion, persists, after due warning, in delaying the play in order to recover his strength or wind, or for any other reason. However, an interval of one minute shall be permitted between games and of two minutes between the fourth and fifth games of a five-games match. A player may leave the court during such intervals, but shall be ready to

esume play at the end of the stated time. Should he fail to do so when required by the referee the match shall be awarded to his opponent.

n the event of play being suspended for the day, the match shall start afresh, unless both players agree to the contrary.

Note to Referees

A player may not open the door or leave the court other than between games without the referee's permission.

22. **Duties of the Marker.** The game is controlled by the marker, who shall call the play and the score. The server's score is called first. He shall call "Fault" (rule 7 (b), (c) and (d)), "Foot Fault" (rule 7 (a)), "Out of Court" or "Not up" as the case may be. If in the course of play the marker calls "Not up" or "Out of Court" the rally shall cease. If the marker's decision is reversed on appeal a "let" shall be allowed except that if the marker fails to call a ball "Not up" or "Out of

Court", and on appeal, it is ruled that such was in fact the case, the stroke shall be awarded accordingly. Any return shall be considered good unless otherwise called.

If after the server has served one fault a "let" is allowed, the marker shall call "One fault" before the server serves again.

When no referee is appointed, the marker shall exercise all the powers of the referee.

23. **The Referee.** A referee may be appointed to whom all appeals shall be directed, including appeals from the marker's decisions and calls. He shall not normally interfere with the marker's calling of the game except:

(a) upon appeal by one of the players;

(b) as provided for in rule 17;

(c) when it is apparent to him that the marker has made a mistake in calling the game.

First Note to Referees

Notwithstanding the above, in the absence of an appeal, if it is

evident that the score has been called incorrectly, the referee shall draw the marker's attention to this fact.

Second Note to Referees

When a decision has been made by the referee, he shall announce it to the players, and the marker shall repeat it with the consequent score, e.g. "Let ball", "no let" or "point to . . .".

24. **Power of the Referee in Exceptional Cases.** The referee has power to order:

(a) A player who has left the court to play on;

(b) A player to leave the court for any reason whatsoever and to award the match to his opponent;

(c) A match to be awarded to a player whose opponent fails to be present in the court within ten minutes of the advertised time of play.

(d) Play to be stopped in order that a player or players may be warned that their conduct on the court is leading to an infringement of the rules.

Note to Referees

A referee should avail himself of this rule as early as possible where one or other of the players is showing a tendency to break the provisions of rule 17.

25. **Colour of Player's Clothing.** Players are required to wear white clothing. The referee's decision thereon to be final.

Appendix I—Definitions

Board. The expression denoting a line, the top edge of which is 19 inches (·483m.) from the floor, set out upon the upper edge of a band of resonant material fixed upon the front wall and extending the full width of the court.

Cut Line. A line set out upon the front wall, six feet (1·829m.) above the floor and extending the full width of the court.

Game Ball. The state of the game when the server requires one point

to win is said to be "Game Ball".

Half-Court Line. A line set out upon the floor parallel to the side walls, dividing the back half of the court into two equal parts called right half court and left half court respectively.

Hand-in. The player who serves.

Hand-out. The player who receives the service.

Hand. The period from the time when a player becomes hand-in until he becomes hand-out.

Not-up. The expression used to denote that a ball has not been returned above the board in accordance with the rules.

Out of Court. The ball is out of court when it touches the front, sides, or back of the court above the area prepared for play or passes over any cross bars or other part of the roof of the court. The lines delimiting such area, the lighting equipment and the roof are out of court.

Service Box or Box. A delimited

area in each half court from within which hand-in serves.

Short Line. A line set out upon the floor parallel to and 18 feet (5·486m.) from the front wall and extending the full width of the court.

Striker. The player whose turn it is to play after the ball has hit the front wall.

Time or Stop. Expression used by the referee to stop play.

Appendix II—Standard Dimensions of a Singles Court

Length: 32 feet (9·75m.)

Breadth: 21 feet (6·40m.)

Height to upper edge of cut line on front wall: 6 feet (1·83m.)

Height to lower edge of front-wall line: 15 feet (4·57m.)

Height to lower edge of back-wall line: 7 feet (2·13m.)

Distance to further edge of short line from front wall: 18 feet (5·49m.)

Height to upper edge of board from ground: 19 inches (·48m.)

Thickness of board (flat or rounded at top): $\frac{1}{2}$ to 1 inch (12$\frac{1}{2}$ to 25mm.)

Height of side-wall line: The diagonal line joining the front-wall line and the back-wall line.

The service boxes shall be entirely enclosed on three sides, within the court by lines, the short line forming the side nearest to the front wall, the side wall bounding the fourth side.

The internal dimensions of the services boxes shall be 5ft. 3in. (1·601m.).

All dimensions in the court shall be measured, where practicable, from the junction of the floor and front wall.

The lines marking the boundaries of the court shall be 2 inches in width (5·0 cm.).

In respect of the outer boundary lines on the walls, it is suggested that the plaster should be so shaped as to produce a concave channel along such lines.

The width of other painted lines shall not exceed 2 inches (5·0 cm.). All walls shall be white or near white. The space below the board shall be white. All lines shall be coloured red.

The front wall shall be of composition. The side walls and back wall shall be of wood or of composition. The floor should be of wood for covered courts and of composition for open courts.

The board and the space below it to the floor and the area above the height of play on the back wall should be constructed of some resonant material.

Appendix III—Dimensions of a Racket

The overall length shall not exceed 27·0 inches or 685 mm. The internal stringing area shall not exceed 8$\frac{1}{2}$ inches or 215 mm. in length by 7$\frac{1}{4}$ inches or 184 mm. in breadth and the framework of the head shall measure not more than 9/16 inch or 14 mm. across the face by 13/16 inch or 20 mm. deep. The framework of the head shall be of wood. The handle shaft shall be made of wood, cane, metal or glass fibre. The grip and foundation may be made of any suitable material.

Appendix IV—Specification for Standard Squash Rackets Balls

The ball must conform to the following:—

1. It must weigh not less than 23·3 grammes and not more than 24·6 grammes (approximately 360-380 grains).

2. Its diameter must be not less than 39·5 mm. and not more than 41·5 mm. (approximately 1·56 to 1·63 inches).

3. It must have a matt surface finish.

4. It must be of a type specifically approved for championship play by

the International Squash Rackets
Federation.

5. Compression Specification:

(i) The ball is mounted in an
apparatus and a load of 0·42 kgm
is applied which deforms the ball
slightly. Subsequent deformation in
the test procedure is measured from
this datum.

(ii) An additional load of 2·4 kgm
is applied and this deforms the ball
further. The deformation from the
datum position is recorded.

(iii) The deformation obtained in
(ii) should be between 3 and 7 mms
for balls of playing properties
acceptable to the I.S.R.F.